What Are You Hungry For?

Body • Mind • Soul

By François Comunetti

Cover Illustration

Painting - *Diaphanie* - by Swiss artist Antoine Oser: Representing Body, Mind and Soul in a universe of dualities.

The word Diaphanie originates from the Greek. In German it means, among other things, translucency or transparency.

Colors and size have been modified with the permission of the artist.

Dedication

To the friends of Philostro

Edited and printed by Bookbaby.com
ISBN# 978-1-66785-727-5
Email: 4windsfarmmt@gmail.com

*Thank you to all who have
helped me write this book.*

To Fred Provenza who inspired me to finally write my book and who pulled the trigger; to my wife Kate who spent many hours correcting and editing; to Gene Gable, who helped on so many levels to put the book together: his professionalism, knowledge, and positive attitude were and are invaluable; to Lupo Perseverando for spiritual guidance; to John Freeman who challenged many of my thoughts; to my brother Philippe for his input and who has an inherent trait for social ethics; to Antoine Oser, who permitted me to use his art work and allowed me to modify it; and finally to Bookbaby.com, a great tool for editing and self-publishing.

Contents

Food for the Body

Food for the Mind

Food for the Soul

Preface

This book is based on personal life experiences, encounters, and observations associated with statements, teachings, and missions from inspiring people. It is also inspired by a lifetime of watching and observing nature, which is the most basic teacher in this world. People who teach us the most and best on the long run are the closest to us—spouse and children, parents—but very often also common unknown people working behind the scenes who have proven through their actions to serve what is Good, Beautiful, and Just for all.

Personally, I was also inspired by professional masters in farming, finances, martial arts, and music. My life crossed paths with mentors like Mrs. Liberman, a martial arts shaman who lived in Paris; with Dan Millman the Peaceful Warrior, but most of all, and still very much to this day, the impact of the most exceptional person, someone I would call the mentor of all mentors and who I never met.

This book is directed mostly to young American adults but will hopefully also help anyone else who is searching for more awareness of their real need for nourishment of their whole being.

I consciously wrote this book in simple words not only to attempt to pass on the message as well as possible but also because of my limitation in the art of writing.

The book is not a source of new knowledge, or a new mission of any kind. The ingredients have been around forever but have been put together in a way to make it palatable, pleasant, and nutritious for people hungry for this kind of food in our present time. We all have different needs.

Consider this book as a kind of tour guide. Finding truth, honest information, and indications suiting our needs become more and more of a dilemma, especially in our times, where we can find a vast range of answers to all our questions online. The more information we can access, the more confusing it gets for some. The more we experience, the more we learn and realize how little we are and how little we know. The more we grow, the less we have an opinion about worldly matters.

As visitors to this planet, we really do not consciously know where we come from and where we are going. The memory and vision of that have been taken from us for the time being here. We can accept explanations provided by science, mythologies or by bright and illuminated or divine people, or just walk by during our distractions and willfully ignore them.

Historically, different cultures transmit wisdom, knowledge, and traditions by word of mouth only and over generations and centuries, such as Native Americans. Some go through scriptures, such as Christians or Muslims. Science proves, evaluates, and duplicates material processes but always ignores the reason. Science knows how but does not know why. This book tries to show that there is no contradiction between science and mythology and that the wall and division between the two is created by us. How can our small and very short-lived brains grasp much, if anything, in limitless space and time?

Let's be humble and admit that we do not really know much, if anything, and therefore, we should be as open-minded as possible to everything presented to us.

Prologue and Life Lessons

What pushed me to write this book?

It was a natural and strong desire to share and pass on what I have learned. Close friends repeatedly asked me to do so. Having lived pretty much isolated in Montana for several years now, the time seemed right as I became hungrier to share this with you. My backpack was becoming heavier; it made no sense to keep carrying experiences around just for myself.

Unfortunately, it is my nature sometimes to be too careful. I take my time to act and even react. If this is the picnic you were looking for on your journey, I am sorry for the delay. I hope it is not too late. Many of us have the impression that we, Homo sapiens, are running out of time. This book starts with my life story and some personal life lessons that I want to share. I am not interested in talking about myself. Still, I want to illustrate with my own experiences that our journeys are not a coincidence. Everything happens for a good reason. Our lives are orchestrated by something much more significant before and beyond us in time and space.

I have been extremely blessed throughout my life, and I am probably the most content presently.

I was born in Switzerland in 1958, in a peaceful and very civilized country. I grew up during a period where life seemed good for just about everyone. There were many doors open for driven people of all occupations and social ranks. Goodwill was, and is, important.

Since early childhood, nature was a compelling attraction for me. Nature without human intervention has always been and still is my principal teacher. As a young child in elementary school, I often woke up early in the morning before class and went running in the woods and through the fields to watch the sunrise.

My father was a nuclear physicist who became a naturalist in his later years. My mother was a well-educated, cultivated, refined French lady attracted by history, culture, fine arts, and high society. She instinctively knew how to raise a family with a lot of wisdom. I was seven years old when my parents got me a violin, hoping that I might make a career out of it. I had an ear for music and was considered gifted. Instead, as a young teenager, I was attracted to martial arts and farming. During my childhood, our family spent every summer vacation in France at my grandparents. They had an oversized lot with a very well-kept vegetable garden. Much of what we ate during the summer came from that garden. I learned a lot from my French grandfather, and I realize how much I learned unconsciously by watching him working in the garden. Meat and fish were from the farmer's market, and a local dairy farmer delivered dairy products. There was no supermarket. Life was simple and good.

Always fascinated by farm life, I sometimes worked during my high school vacations on farms for just room and board and a little pocket money. I always liked to be active in sports. For a while, I fantasized about becoming a professional boxer. However, I never told my parents. I realized the cultural disconnect with my family. I quickly gave up on that idea because I also knew it was a very violent sport, and that I had no right to destroy the gift of a good and healthy body. Instead, I picked up Judo, which I knew was acceptable to my parents. I never quit Judo, and to this very day, I am still on the mat twice a week assisting teenage boys with life lessons learned within this martial art. I was fourteen years old when I put on a Judo Gi for the first time. As I walked into the dojo, I knew this activity would be a long journey and an essential part of my life.

For a long time, I looked up to my Sensei as to a god. He was a tall, athletic, and intelligent man with charisma. He won the Swiss National Title in the heavy-weight category seven times. He also ranked on the international level. Is it a coincidence that the day I felt like writing about him was the day he passed, as I found out later from his wife? Thank you, Leo! It is also no coincidence that I had the urge to visit with him during my last trip to Switzerland, as I had not seen Sensei Leo for twenty years.

As a child, I never really knew why I went to school, but I enjoyed it most of the time. The last couple of years of high school did not go very well, so I advanced my mandatory military service and served as a cyclist/bazooka shooter.

My father, an open-minded person who could think outside the box, took my counselor's advice at that time. He found a farm on the Lake of Geneva where I could begin an apprenticeship in organic farming. Pierre, the owner and a master farmer, was a pioneer in organic agriculture in Switzerland. He had farmed organically since the sixties. I was delighted. Not to mention that one of the best Judo schools in Switzerland was in bicycle range, as I had neither car nor license at that time. It was perfection, and I had everything I needed for a while.

I worked twelve hours/day on the farm, and before dinner, I jumped on my military bicycle to go to Judo. The Judo classes were high performance, and I achieved the National Level as a junior. Between hard farm labor and Judo, it is unbelievable what I asked my body to do at this period in my life. Looking back, I would not do it again. I would offer my body more rest. No wonder a few years later, my body did resign for a while due to exhaustion.

Before finishing my two years of farmer apprenticeship, I decided to go to Canada to work in the logging business. I fantasized about being lost in the middle of Canada, far away from any civilization, logging hard and experiencing a natural, intense, and physical life out in the wilderness. Of course, it turned out differently, but better. Instead, I stayed with Vincent, an ex-military buddy from Switzerland in Toronto, for one month. It was a sabbatical for me, enjoying plenty of free time, something lacking or nonexistent on the farm. I continued to work out twice a day, did my morning runs, and in the evening, Judo practice at the best school in Toronto. There I had a humbling lesson. Although I was quite strong in mat work in Switzerland, I got whipped by a world-class fighter. His name was Vargas, and though he was a weight category above me, it was an important lesson and experience at the right time.

One month later, Vincent decided to move to San Diego, California, with his old Buick Skylark. I thought it would be fun and exciting to join him. What an adventure it was for me coming from little Switzerland! It was like turning livestock loose on the pasture in Spring after spending the winter cooped up inside.

After visiting San Diego, I returned to Nebraska, where I had met a gorgeous local girl on my way to the West Coast. Of course, I loved San Diego's beaches, but I was more attracted by the Midwest's vast farming area and knew that was more where I belonged. Looking back, it was no coincidence; this beautiful young lady lured me back to Nebraska for a reason and dumped me soon after I arrived. Within a couple of days, I found a perfect farm growing hundreds of acres of grain. So, I spent the summer working on this grain farm. When entering Nebraska, the State sign says "Nebraska – The Good Life," which I experienced. I was blessed to stay with the wonderful owners of the farm, Ray, and Rita.

By Fall, I went back to Switzerland to attend an agricultural school. This school, the "Farmer-Winter-School," is designed for future farm-owners or managers. This was the best school I ever attended or could even imagine. There were approximately 150 young farmers all driven with an entrepreneurial spirit, most of them living on campus. The subjects taught at this farmer school were very practically oriented and useful. The principal, Mr. Bachman, was an outstanding person with an incredible memory. On the first day of school, he called to me across the hall by my name. I had never seen or talked to him before that! No one ever failed his class in bookkeeping and farm economy.

Anyone who did not pass a test had the opportunity to do the same test again the next day during dinner time but with a maximum possible 80 percent score. How ingenious! Three life lessons in one, in a very human way!

In spring, when school ended for the year, I just had to go back to America, but now, I wanted to work on a dairy farm. A school buddy had the same plan, so off we went. We both ended up in Wisconsin on different dairy operations, both working for expatriated Swiss families. We were so hungry for discovery in the profession and new dimensions that we worked twelve hours a day just for room and board and a little pocket money. Joe Lauper, the owner of a good-sized dairy operation at the time, taught me how to work efficiently, with minimum investment, and how to stay out of debt. Needless to say, he survived every farm economy crisis.

You must understand that many Swiss people have a strong urge to travel and explore. Switzerland is a tiny and densely populated country with very high cultural requirements. The society does not leave much room for error. The expectations are high. Therefore, young people, especially young men, are fascinated by big countries with lots of physical and cultural space and tolerance. America and Canada were perfect for that and quite popular travel destinations in the eighties and nineties. They were still lands of endless opportunities.

Quite a few Swiss farmers even sold their properties in Switzerland during that time. They immigrated to Canada, the United States, and Australia to acquire much bigger places with the sale of their small and high-priced farms in Switzerland.

I was a farmer without land. After my dairy experience and more traveling across the United States with my friend John in his junker Ford Matador, I went back to Switzerland to finish the farmer school. After that, I took a job working in the vineyards for a major winery on Lake Geneva.

After harvest in the fall, I decided to get more fully into Judo. I hoped to rise to an international level. I could not afford Japan, so I went to what was comparable in excellence: The INSEP in Paris. A friend of my parents offered me a room at the Place de Clichy in downtown Paris. My roommate was a refugee from Laos.

My routine was to get up at 5 a.m., before traffic, and jog up to Montmartre, the hill of the martyrs. The last one-fourth mile consists of stairs and leads up to a massive and dominant church, which looks more like the US Capitol building. It was perfect for an excellent early morning run that ended up overlooking Paris. I jumped like Sylvester Stallone in the movie Rocky with fantasies of future glory. Later in the morning, I lifted weights, and by mid-afternoon, I jumped on the Metro to be at the INSEP on the outskirts of Paris at 4 p.m. There were about seventy to eighty world-class black belts from several different countries. Wow, "plenty of meat," as we say in Judo slang in Europe! I had also worked with Thierry Rey, the current gold medalist in my weight category. Not to mention that the second week I got to Paris, I also met a nice girl who also practiced Judo regularly. I was in Heaven.

My plans changed after only three weeks when I injured my back seriously enough to stop my workouts temporarily. It was not an unfortunate "accident" or a bad coincidence but an invitation and opportunity to pay attention to other things in life, which were more critical. It put me on the journey I was supposed to take.

My landlord Simon Levy, who provided a free room for me and had done so for Laotian refugees, was the kind of man everybody wanted to see and talk to. He was working independently in his office, managing the finances of wealthy people. Outside of his working hours, there were constantly all kinds of people going in and out of his office, asking for help or advice in life: driven businesspeople, students, parents in crises with their teenagers, unemployed, homeless, prostitutes, and drug addicts. He listened and encouraged them all because they kept coming back. He emanated compassion and love in the most captive way and was always fully present when somebody talked to him. With few words and a contagious fire inside him, he inspired his visitors, mostly younger people. He made you immediately decide to turn your life around in a good way and do the right thing. The first time I introduced Simon to my wife several years later, his loving presence immediately brought tears to her eyes.

I was an injured Judo Ka, unexpectedly confronting my broken dreams. I did not know what to do with my life at that moment. I was lost in a world of endless opportunities, except for the one I wanted so badly. So, I spent a short while every day with Simon in his office for the rest of my stay. He recommended, and just about convinced me, to go back to college, and get an additional degree in agriculture, since I had no land of my own. That was the very last thing I wanted to do; anything but go back to school! During that same period, my Parisian girlfriend, Veronique, gave me a book written by Mrs. Jeanne Liberman. Today, I would call her an exceptionally gifted Master or Shaman. The book was in French and titled something like Old Age is a Myth or Old Age Does Not Exist. I read the book and was fascinated, especially since she started Judo at age fifty-three, became a black belt five years later, and achieved a black belt in Aikido as well. I called her up, and by some miracle, she accepted a personal consultation with me. A little lady in her upper eighties opened the door. "Come on in and sit down." Then nothing. After a little while of silence. . . "What's up?" Surprised by what I felt was a cold reception, I explained my life situation for half an hour. I made her understand that I felt a little lost and did not know where to go with my life and wondered how she could help me. I expected her to tell me what direction I should go and what to do and not do.

She had listened attentively without any interruption, and after I finished, she looked at me for a few more seconds and then said: "Well, If you want to do something, do it, if not, don't!". . . followed by a very uncomfortable and awkward long pause for me, and then she said: "Anything else?". . . Wow! Talk about a cold shower. But this was EXACTLY what I needed to hear! It ignited something in me. As the "anything else" I mentioned that I injured my back at Judo. "Let me see" and she lifted my T-shirt and put her fingers right on the spot. "I see," she said and went gently back and forth with her fingers two or three times. "You will be fine, but be careful for a while." I wanted to offer her some money for the counseling session, but she refused categorically. Then, she accompanied me to the door. I was still hoping for some magic words of wisdom coming out at the last second. But nothing, nada! Years later, I realized that what she had said was a whole lot and precisely what I needed to hear!

Jumping onto the Metro, I found a seat with a heating pipe running through the back cushion, or so I thought. As it felt so warm at one spot, I moved forward and touched the seat, which was cold, to my surprise. Yet, it felt like somebody was pressing a warm, almost hot sponge right where my back injury was and where Mrs. Liberman had set her fingers. Thank you, Mrs. Liberman! One sentence and a few seconds of treatment healed my body and mind and gave me a new direction in Life. My Judo accident was for a perfect reason.

When back in Switzerland, I began a temporary job trucking fruits in barrels from farms to a distillery that belonged to the National Swiss Junior Judo team's coach. I unconsciously was still resisting going back to school. The boss offered me room and board, knowing that I was serious about Judo and work. Moving the fifty-gallon fruit barrels and daily Judo was hard work, and just the way I usually liked it. Not for long. Thankfully, life orchestrated something against my will and for my higher good. Typically, after age twenty-four, things will become difficult if you have unfinished business in your twelve-year cycles. I was told this once by a friend of my father's, and which was precisely my experience.

I started to feel limits to my energy; I had a continuous cold and sore throat and was no longer energetic. I often woke up in a sweat at night. One day, instead of going to Judo, I decided to skip my workout, relax a little, and take in a movie instead. While driving to town, my legs became heavy. The road was going in and out of focus in an elastic back and forth motion. I could not make it to the theater and had to pull over. My heart began to beat very Irregularly with long pauses in between. I almost passed out. So, I crawled out of the car and waved to the one behind me, which stopped to my surprise. I asked the young couple to take me to the emergency room and told them that I was not sure I would make it, which I honestly believed. I thought, "That's it; my heart has had enough of my abuse and is going to stop. Life puts a stop to that behavior." The couple was anxious and rushed me to the hospital. Their compassion felt good and gave me hope. I was able to walk into the emergency room with the help of that young couple. Once I collapsed on the rolling stretcher, I knew I was in good hands and was going to make it. I was able to let go instantly. For one reason or another, I fully trusted the process. What else could I have done?

After three weeks of full rest ordered by the doctor and after the doctors had found nothing wrong with me except exhaustion, life came slowly back into me, and it felt good. But one night, during these three weeks, I woke up again in a cold sweat with an irregular heartbeat. I was staying at my lovely sister's, who was a nurse, but did not want to wake anybody and get them to panic. So instead, I took my responsibilities and had a face-to-face with the situation and my current life and asked Heaven for help and asked what life wanted from me. What was continually present in my mind and which I refused for too long became inevitable. The next thing I knew, I had finally decided at that moment to go back to college, which was the last thing I wanted to do until then. It was against my will, but apparently, Life required that from me. In one way, I felt like a dog or horse giving in, bowing its head down after losing a confrontation, and in another way, I felt very relieved. I finally gave in to my stubbornness and decided to do what life was asking me to do. My crises were for a good reason, no coincidence!

I went back home to stay with my parents. I had left home several years before and going back was tough. It humbled me, to be honest.

During that transition time, I finally asked my dad for the book about Philostro. Since I was a young child,

I knew about this book but was not ready for it until then. I consciously did not want to read it before, because I knew that we are responsible for what we know. When I decided to be more accountable, it was the time for it.

After studying introductory college-level science courses by myself for a few months, I miraculously passed my college admission exam. The Tropical Agricultural Institute prepared students to become engineer-technicians in agriculture. Less than three years later, I graduated. It was one of the proudest moments in my life. Two professors, one the director of organic farming in Switzerland, congratulated me on my diploma work. My thesis was, "How to combat wind and soil erosion in the US Midwest."

The conclusion (and essential life lesson) from this newly achieved milestone for me was apparent. What you want to do the least is often what you need to do the most. Life will lead you to what you are supposed to do; we then receive the assistance necessary. Today, I am sure of that assistance. It is guaranteed! I also learned that mishaps and accidents happen for very good reasons. They lead us onto a better path, and we become stronger and more compassionate. I discovered that, of all the things we need to accomplish during the day or in our lives, what must be done first is what is in front of us, sometimes the thing we want to do least. Though indeed this seems often difficult, it is what we should fully embrace.

"Start by doing what's necessary, then do what's possible; and suddenly you are doing the impossible."

–Saint Francis of Assisi

Right after college, I met Dr. Elisabeth Kubler-Ross, a Swiss doctor and author. She wrote several books that broke the taboo on death and dying in America's medical field at that time. She also started the hospice movement. After a short discussion, she invited me to work on her farm in Virginia during the summer. She also recommended that I assist some of her workshops. I was thrilled. A few weeks later, on a Saturday afternoon in March, I arrived by hitchhiking the last few miles to her farm. As was often the case, Elisabeth was abroad, so the current farm manager welcomed me. There were already visitors. One of them was a retired coal miner who was, a few years prior, trapped for many days with some coworkers in a Pennsylvania mine accident. In their desperation, they had a mysterious apparition to support and encourage the crew. He wanted to share his experience with Elisabeth.

As we talked by the cozy wood stove, a young and attractive lady named Kate walked in and served us tea, cheese, and crackers. Kate has been my wife for over twenty-eight years now. But that did not happen right away. She arrived in Virginia from Alaska three days before me. Was that a coincidence? I do not think so. It was as if "somebody" arranged it. We immediately hit it off and enjoyed working on the farm together. It felt very good being around her and working with her. I assume it was mutual, as impressions we have about other people usually are.

Unfortunately, my wild cowboy spirit was not quite ready to settle down. I was not ready to be responsible. So, I let her go back to her job in Alaska about a month later as she had initially planned, but I shouldn't have. Before Kate left, Elisabeth suggested I marry Kate and that we stay and manage her farm. It was not a suggestion out of the blue by a random person. It came from a lady with plenty of experience, wisdom, and deep insight into life. I should have listened. That was the first indication.

On a Sunday morning, I got up right before dawn and went out to absorb the peace and serenity of this beautiful place. It was a magical moment, and it felt like Heavenly entities were very present. The Creator imposed Himself with His masterpiece, the beauty of Nature, which automatically invited me to connect, meditate, and pray. I asked in my prayer if Kate would be the right woman for me as I have always been slow

17

to make decisions. As I continued, I asked myself when and if I would have an answer? I kept walking, and minutes later, as I looked around, I saw Kate sitting on top of a little hill, apparently also in admiration of the beauty and peace of that morning. I walked up to her and said: "Admiring this beautiful morning and praising the Creator?" "Very much so," she confirmed, and I immediately knew that I had an answer to my question. That was the second indication. I did not tell her about my thoughts because I was not ready. I was not going to have any attachments. Why? Years later, I realized that my desire to remain "free" was due to a lack of forgiveness to previous failed relationships.

A few days later, I lost my glasses, the only pair I ever lost in my life. I have worn glasses since the age of seven. We looked everywhere, and Kate helped me. Elisabeth told me later that day: "Obviously, there is something you don't want to see." Unfortunately, and only much later, I realized this was the third indication. I never found the glasses.

A couple of weeks after that, I recall watching Kate take off in a little airplane out of Staunton, Virginia, heading back to Alaska. I kept looking at the plane, as long as I could, until it disappeared into the clouds. My state of mind and heart were divided. The next time I saw her again was five years later when I picked her up at a small airport in Switzerland. Our life story resumed where it had stopped.

After Kate left Virginia, I remained in America for almost two years. After I left Elisabeth's farm, I was fortunate to find work with one of the best purebred sheep breeders in the country, Ansel & Carol Luxford. They started out in Virginia, ended up in Wyoming, and later Montana. Some of the highest priced Suffolk rams came out of their operation. Ansel Luxford earned entry into the Suffolk Sheep Breeders Hall of Fame in 2017. I then went back to Switzerland while enjoying my "freedom." But soon, I had the impression that I was turning in circles on several levels. It was an exciting time, but I got tired of it and was looking for more. I wanted to be responsible and wanted to have a family. Also, I finally accepted and realized a statement of Philostro: "The purpose of marriage is not to be happy, but to evolve and grow mutually."

I made a list of the best women I had met in the past years. Kate was on top of the list. I had only talked with her once by telephone since we parted. I decided to write my first letter to her, which was still a popular thing to do in 1991. I asked her straight out if she was interested in raising a family with me on a farm. She replied by letter very soon and suggested that she certainly would love to come for a visit. To my surprise, she was still single and hadn't had a steady relationship since I met her. I bought her an airplane ticket, and one month later, I picked her up at the local airport.

Three months later, we got married; the first time a civil ceremony in Los Angeles with her family and one month later in a religious ceremony in Switzerland with mine.

We decided to settle in France and associate with a dairy farmer. Our cultural differences were a challenge, especially for my wife, who had never lived in a foreign country for a more extended time. We are now grateful for that challenge, and we see it as an extremely valuable asset. Cultural differences add additional challenges and values to married life. It is wise to follow the author Antoine de St. Exupery's advice, best known for writing The Little Prince. "Love does not consist of gazing at each other, but in looking outward together in the same direction."

The price of my delay in deciding to marry Kate had a high cost. Philostro once said that time is precious and that we should not waste it. I also recall reading in The Way of the Peaceful Warrior by Dan Millman, that this life does not always give us a second chance. I came to realize that. Being in our mid-thirties, an age with reduced fertility for most women, we were never able to have our own children. We also did not believe in forcing the issue with modern medical processes that were available then. We certainly did everything else to optimize the chances. Still, we trusted and worked with God and Nature and asked Heaven for help. Help came, but different than we expected.

We adopted three boys in the most mysterious way and were very clearly guided during the process. Kate does not appear to be particularly religious but has a strong spiritual connection or attraction to the Virgin Mary. Three years into our marriage, Kate had a part-time job at a butcher shop. She had cleaned the glass countertop before opening the shop to customers. But before opening the door, she discovered a small Lourdes medal on the counter, even though no one had entered after she cleaned the counter. Previously, we had begun to look into adoption. We had received an address of a couple in the southwest of France who could maybe help us find children to adopt. After Kate told me that she found a Lourdes medal at the store that day, and could not explain how it got there, I suggested making a trip to southwestern France. We would combine both visits. First, to the shrine of Our Lady of Lourdes to ask for help with children. Next, we would visit the couple who were living just about an hour's drive away.

On September 13th, we were in Lourdes, asking Heaven for guidance. We were not aware that this is a significant date for Mary's apparitions. The same evening, we met the Latvian/French couple, who showed us pictures of many children in orphanages in the Baltic States. Overwhelmed, Kate and I went for a walk that evening, where we enjoyed a fabulous meteorite shower for over an hour. I told Kate that one boy in the pictures struck me because I thought he looked like a little American boy. The lady had no idea if this boy was available for adoption. Many children are in orphanages in these countries because their families are too poor to take care of them. Still, they will eventually reunite with them. About one month later, Inta called us and said that this boy was up for adoption. After the legal process and all the paperwork were complete, we went to pick up Marc. He arrived at our house in Switzerland on June 13th, exactly nine months after our request in Lourdes and seeing his picture for the first time on that same evening.

We also hoped to adopt his two full-blood brothers. But we had neither the money, space, nor time. We both had jobs as well as livestock to tend to.

It is in Swiss people's nature to be very careful and not take unnecessary risks in life. Family, colleagues, and friends warned us that this could be very risky for us on several levels, primarily because of our financial situation at the time. But we jumped into it with both feet. When we started the adoption process for Marc's brothers, they were seven and eight years old. Without asking, help came from everywhere and out of the blue. I received a significant raise in pay. We got an offer for housing in a beautiful farmhouse constructed in 1684 overlooking the Lake of Geneva with land and fruit trees around it, for half the rent initially requested. We were gifted a reliable car to drive to Latvia to pick up the two brothers. Our current vehicle would not have made the 3,000-mile trip. An unexpected double sub-sidy came in from the State for the adoption of two kids at once. As a family deal, health insurance fees dropped considerably and were even free of cost after one year. Two days after the boys arrived, Luc fractured his arm. Health Insurance coverage had not yet taken effect, so a charity foundation covered hospital costs. The land-lord of my father's office, a wealthy man, supported our adoption decision. He released a considerable amount of cash over the next few years for our family.

We were not rich by any means, but felt like it; rich in blessings and assistance from Above. How could we ignore that life is orchestrated from behind the scenes and that we have to "trust the process?" I also recalled both of my grandmothers saying independently: "The children come with their package," meaning, when they arrive in this world, they bring with them what they need for their journey. I also recalled Philostro saying that we are not supposed to worry or ask Heaven for material goods; it is already taking care of at birth.

My dream of owning a farm was still very present, but it would take a few more years to come to fruition. Though I already had a few cattle in Switzerland, I did not have any land and had to lease everything from land to equipment. Besides, I had a full-time job at a winery. After nine years, I got laid off, and it was an invitation to change our course in life.

Kate always had the urge to go back to the United States to take care of her mother, who lived alone in a suburb of Los Angeles. I was very hesitant. We had a great life in Switzerland, and I was sure that I would find another good job soon. Kate waited for my response for a couple of months. For her birthday, I chose a card with a US flag on it and wrote: Let's go! By summer, the whole family was in LA at Grandma's. It was an exciting move and sad at the same time, leaving my family and friends. I also recall watching heavy-heartedly the truck driving away from the farm with my cattle sold. I might never farm again or might never have cows again, I remember thinking at that moment, especially moving to LA! But I knew it was for a bigger purpose.

Being busy settling down in the City of Angels, after two months, I thought it was time to find a job. Without any résumé, I spontaneously walked down to a commercial area a few blocks away with absolutely nothing to show in my hands. I asked to talk to the manager of a supermarket. At midnight, I started to work as a clerk in the wine section.

A few months later, my sister, who lived in Switzerland, met a US broker who said their Trading Company in LA was hiring. Working in a financial brokerage firm was about the last thing I wanted to do. But feeling obligated to follow up on it while raising a family, I sent out a very simple quarter-page résumé by Fax! The next day the phone rang, and I said to my wife, "I know who is calling, and I do not want that job." After several rings, I picked up the phone anyway, and the brokerage firm invited me for an interview. I went with the idea of doing this as an exercise and wouldn't have to accept the job. I did not worry about the interview, as I did not really care to be hired. Among the questions at the interview was: "What does money mean to you?" I thought I would tell him spontaneously what I believe and could care less if it was the answer he expected. I said: "Well, to me, it is just a form of energy which one must handle carefully." It was quiet for a while, and I thought, okay, I am off the hook. Then I was asked: "What would you do to make good money?" I understood nothing about trading the markets, so I thought this answer would release me from being hired: "Work hard," I said. Management liked my answers, and I started as a broker assistant at 6 a.m. the next morning. I realized this was all meant to be.

In the first couple of weeks, I asked myself what the hell I was doing there. A year and a half later, I passed my broker license, one of the proudest moments in my life. Today, I still take more pride in being a broker than in being a farmer.

Looking back, I realized again how things seem to be orchestrated from out of sight. Also, I realized that very often, what we want to do the least is what we need to do the most. After three to four years, I started to make good money, which was indispensable for our boys' education. My dream of a farm was out of sight. However, I had the opportunity to grow a big vegetable garden near our house on an empty lot, a very prime spot just nine miles from downtown LA! People walking by often said: "I can't believe this still exists in LA!" We even had a few chickens in the backyard and planted a few fruit trees and grapevines.

Our boys did not adapt well to suburban Los Angeles, coming from a rural and tame area in Switzerland. We warned them early on that we would not tolerate any marijuana smoking and absolutely no other drugs. We also had them sign a contract with a tremendous financial incentive if they abstained from smoking and drinking until high school graduation. It did not work. Like many parents, we had a few fundamental principles about raising kids. Now we had a few boys but no more principles. We decided to send our boys to a ranch in Montana, where these institutions are called "programs." It cost us a fortune, but the money came in on time. We had a lot of respect for that program, as we thought the owners managed it very well in a small family setting. Teenage boys enjoyed a simpler life and had to earn all privileges, including going to public school. We came to realize that parents and society are at least as responsible for the problems as the kids themselves. We were undoubtedly also partially to blame and noticed that these programs help the parents as well. They are a big release for the whole family. I believe this respite can save marriages, though about 85 percent of these kids come from broken homes anyway. So, life was better and more manageable now in beautiful Southern California, with the drama of adolescence temporarily removed. I recall saying to my wife one fall,

"Well, I guess our farm is going to be a very little one right here; let's improve our backyard more, plant a couple more fruit trees and do our best with what we have."

A couple of months later, I got a call from the program owner, saying that I should visit my boys again. They had left the program after graduating; they were over eighteen and were living in that area. Shortly after I arrived, the owner mentioned that the neighboring ranch was for sale, and I should consider buying it. Surprised, I looked silently at him for a while, totally unprepared for thoughts like that. The farm idea was on the back burner and hardly in my mind anymore. My mother-in-law had passed away a few months prior, and we were now the owners of her house in Los Angeles. Anyway, I spontaneously said: "Let's go look at it." The place was too big for us. After I called my wife to tell her about it, she went online. When I returned home, she was excited to show me another farm for sale in the area that matched all of the requirements we once had listed years ago. As we looked at it together on the website, it clicked for both of us: "That's what we are looking for, that really could be it."

Six months later, we moved to Montana. My brokerage firm allowed me to work from home as a branch office, which required passing another exam. I ran my little one-person brokerage office in the mornings and farmed in the afternoons and weekends. We bought cows, equipment, and we are now selling organic grass-fed/grass-finished beef.

Besides that, I finally started my Judo school, another dream that had been on the back burner for a long time. Twice a week, I am on the Judo mat with a dozen teenage boys. I can say that all of my dreams came true. My wife and I are so grateful to live a life of such abundance in an environment of total beauty.

I recall what the Peaceful Warrior told me twelve years before all that happened: "Keep your dreams in mind." He also illustrated to me that life is often like traveling the roads on the western Plains. Roads that stretch over long distances with small ups and downs throughout the open spaces, where bison once roamed. At the bottom, you can't see far, and you are not sure where you are. Once on top, everything opens up and reveals itself.

I recall something Philostro repeated over and over again. It is something I have known since adolescence and have been consciously working on ever since. It must have made a difference in my life, but it is quite a challenge and just about impossible to accomplish. He so often said: "Refrain from saying anything bad about anybody." He added: "If you make true efforts in that direction, life will not withhold any of your wishes."

We may believe that or not, but isn't it worth a try? I think this effort should not be to serve ourselves, but as a kindness for the good of all. But there is a price to pay. It often makes you look stupid in this world. It means you can barely participate in talks of politics and economy, for example. People will think you are dull. Does it matter? Not as long as it is beneficial to all of us and that it is for a higher purpose. It seems as if the more we work on these kinds of issues, and the more we do for Truth, the lonelier we become in this world. Bon voyage.

Who was Philostro?

When I was young, I can recall several visits to our home by some second-generation followers of an unknown, very exceptional, and mysterious man. I will call him Philostro. He lived in France from the mid-nineteenth century to the beginning of the twentieth century. Locally, he was also called Father of the Poor and was also known as the Counselor of Kings.

I had the great opportunity to meet, among those visitors to my parent's home, Mr. Emil. He was one of the few people still alive whose time on earth coincided with the last years of Philostro. Mr. Emil did not meet him personally but knew about him through relatives who had spent much time with this intriguing man. He married a lady who was from the same small town as Philostro. Mr. Emil was also a co-author of a biography of him.

Philostro was born at the foot of the Alps in Haute Savoy. At age fourteen, he left home on foot for Lyon, a city over fifty miles away. There he helped his uncle, a butcher, to put himself through school. Later, as a medical student and after working in a hospital, Philostro was expelled from school. He had to go to court many times for the "illegal" practice of medicine. His supernatural gift of instant healing was considered illegal. He cured everything from acute diseases to chronic handi-caps.

For example, Philostro saw a soldier crying in his hospital bed because the doctors were going to ampu-tate his leg the next day due to advanced gangrene. Philostro told him that it would not happen, that his leg would heal, but to remain silent about it. The next day, the day of surgery, the surgeon discovered that the gan-grenous flesh was gone. Surgery was canceled, and the soldier healed entirely in a short time. The doctors asked the patient what he did or what had happened. And despite Philostro's request, he said, "It was that short young man with the dark brown hair who did it."

Of course, these kinds of repeated events were, as it still would be today, a big challenge and a thorn in the eye of traditional medicine.

There are records of many of these supernatural healings. They were recorded in city halls, under oath, and with witnesses, officially stamped and signed by the mayor: lame people who suddenly walked, long-term and severe chronic diseases instantly cured, etc.

Philostro could also read people's thoughts; know what they did in their past, and what they did in their previous lives. Once, a tall, healthy, and arrogant police agent said to him in court: "I challenge you to do any-thing you can to me." The man instantly collapsed unconscious. One time, Philostro quietly lit his pipe with a match during a violent wind, while those beside him struggled to keep their hats on.

In Russia, by personal invitation of the Czar, he was questioned by officials about his ability to heal. Philostro asked them to provide him with several random bed numbers in a hospital in St. Petersburg. This hospital was days of travel away, a place Philostro had never officially visited. He provided the proper diagnoses of these patients correctly, and they were subsequently all cured after that.

The saying goes that no one is a prophet in his own country; neither was Philostro. With an education in medicine, he was banned from working in the hospital where he resided in France and had apparently about sixty court sessions with fines. Russia, though, awarded him an honorary degree in medicine. The University in Cincinnati, Ohio, awarded him a degree for his work on hygienic practices at the time of birth.

Philostro held daily sessions for years in the afternoon. All kinds of people with all sorts of physical and mental health and life problems came to these sessions. Before each session, he requested everyone to get up, pray, and ask Heaven for healing. Some of these immediate and spontaneous cures were so unbelievable that some questioned if he was a reincarnation of an apostle or even wondered if he was Christ himself. To that, he answered: "Don't be mistaken, I am nothing, I am the least among you. I am the dog of the shepherd."

He was always incredibly kind and polite to everyone. Somehow, he remained relatively incognito in history. Rasputin, instead, the next adviser to the Czar, is much more recognized today. However, popularity is no indication of the real quality of a person. Hardly anyone knows of Philostro today, just as almost no one knows about Francis Schlatter, who cured thousands in Colorado around the same time.

For most folks, these types of extraordinary people are just too much to handle or believe. We all have the God-given gift of freely choosing our beliefs.

Food for the Body

Today's Confusion about Food

Healthily feeding our bodies was undoubtedly less complicated for Westerners before the industrialization of agriculture. If there was a problem, it was mostly about scarcity or a lack of variety or hygiene. Food was usually nutritious and ordinarily free of toxins. People ate mostly very locally grown and unprocessed foods without any industrial additions.

Processing was drying, smoking, and salting, methods that had been around forever. Canning and pasteurizing came later but were still simple procedures without any additives. Preparing a meal took more time; it was "slow food." The cost of groceries in the family budget was much higher. Drawbacks caused by natural contaminations of foods, such as salmonella in animal products, or the cycle of different types of worms between livestock and people, were more frequent than today.

At the same time, a significant majority of people were thinner and tougher. Looking at pictures through American history to this day, it is undeniable that our society is overweight. People had a healthy weight up to the early seventies. Look at pictures of the youth during the Woodstock era. The dramatic change started shortly after this period. Today, people barely know where their food comes from. How did all this happen?

Unlimited Offerings and Variety

Today in America, it is possible to eat just about anything from any country, culture, or era. In addition to all these possibilities, there are continuously newly developed processed foods and beverages. All of these ultra-processed foods have a long list of ingredients, which only adds to the confusion. Almost every day, we hear about new health scares or health discoveries. Often, we read new claims of natural power foods, which have always existed, by the way. We can find new and ever-changing recipes. To better understand the unlimited offers and endless food combinations (despite quality), compare it with the following illustration:

A significant part of the world population has a telephone number based on just ten digits. This illustrates that with only ten different essential ingredients combined and cooked in various ways, there are almost as many recipes as people in the world. The average human mental capacity is relatively limited and can't handle too much information. To a great extent, the brain becomes more of a handicap when it comes to nourishing our bodies properly. Any life form, from bacteria to mammals instinctively knows what to eat without thinking about it. Yet, they eat healthily.

Our society is confused and lost when it comes to nutrition. Consequently, many people give up their power or intuition to the food industry, medical advice, or doctors. Our brains have partially worked against our interest by taking precedence over our senses: smelling, tasting, and gut feeling. As Dr. Fred Provenza clearly explains in his seminars and his book Nourishment, we can learn from herbivores and omnivores. They show us how to nourish ourselves properly and live within our surrounding landscapes. Yes, we can learn from cows, goats, sheep, and pigs, which roam freely and access natural food choices. They know what is right for them if given a choice.

Why is this? Compared to humans, they barely use their eyes to choose feed. They rely more on smell, flavor, and memory, which unconsciously recalls that choice's effect. No reflection is involved. Our society's hyper-intellectualization and loss of working and living with our landscapes result in a lack of connection to our meant-to-be food sources. This disconnect dispels common sense and creates confusion. Unfortunately, our culture does not recognize the value of our relationship to local landscapes. We have also lost touch with our innate palate and gut wisdom.

Today, our food industry tricks our palates with artificial flavors and sweeteners, which tell lies to our brains. It misleads us about nutrients that are barely present or not present at all. It is comparable to receiving paychecks of little value. Consequently, our bodies say "not enough" and ask for more. We end up with wallets stuffed with worthless paychecks. Think overweight!

Consequences of Industrial Food

Today, most farmland in America is part of the industrial agri-business complex we have created. Developed industrial countries, especially America, have unlimited food supply with an insane variety of nutrient-depleted processed foods. Research shows that our produce, dairy, meat, and eggs have lost between 10 and 50 percent of their nutritional value over the past four decades! This significant and basic fact is very well documented by D.R.Davis, M.D., & H.D.Riordan (2004): Changes in USDA food composition data for 43 garden crops, 1950 to 1999. The Journal of the American College of Nutrition, 23, pp. 669–682.

Mayer, A.-M. (1997). Historical changes in the mineral content of fruits and vegetables. British Food Journal, 99, pp. 207–211.

As a shocking example and to illustrate the overall picture, let's take a conventional mass-produced cherry pie sold in the supermarket today. There can be a direct and indirect exposure of up to approximately 200 chemicals in the basic production of wheat, other grains, eggs, cherries, and sugar. That is in addition to a list of unfamiliar additives shown in the ingredients of the pie itself. It starts with treating wheat seeds with fungicides and continues with field treatments of herbicides and fungicides. Cherry orchards are sprayed even more frequently with insecticides and fungicides. Wheat flour contains additives also. Cherries go through several processes before being bleached and artificially recolored again. Eggs come from medicated chickens that eat genetically modified organisms (GMO)/glyphosate and fungicide treated grains. Also, the assembled ingredients come from various locations in the country or the world.

Before industrialization, cherry pie ingredients were wheat-flour, cherries, butter, salt, cane sugar, and eggs. Luckily, it is still possible in America to make a simple pie with organic ingredients. One can find something very similar at a farmer's market or in a store selling quality food, but it is by far not the norm.

Bread used to contain flour, water, yeast, and salt. Today, the list of ingredients in a conventional loaf of white bread is full of chemicals unknown to the public. Recently, I was offered a beautiful-looking piece of chocolate cake from the supermarket, which tasted pretty good: picture/copy of label:

Watching T.V. programs about industrial agriculture and listening to these farmers' and technicians' suggestions on managing crops is like listening to chemists. Indeed, an occasional treatment that saves a crop or an adjustment with a synthetic fertilizer when soil becomes depleted of a specific nutrient is helpful. Using chemicals in agriculture can be compared to treating disease by medicating the symptoms and then demanding more treatments due to the ensuing side effects. This approach is a failure to address the real problem. As a society based on consumerism, be it in medicine or agriculture, the first solution is often adding something, be it a pill or a chemical treatment.

It is much more effective to remove something, like not overfeeding or intoxicating our bodies or the soil, in most cases. Our American culture has not yet discovered the advantage and benefits of restriction. It is just not popular. Most of us prefer to keep eating and drinking without restriction. We then need to take blood pressure medication or antacids, which then cause side effects that must be treated also.

The first and most fundamental mistake of industrial agriculture is massive synthetic fertilizing. It is junk food for soil and plants and creates a form of addiction. The biggest offender is nitrogen fertilizer. Besides diluting the nutrients in produce, it slows soil microorganisms' activity and depletes the soil of organic matter. The excess quantities are washed into the groundwater and end up in the rivers and oceans. A study done at the University of Michigan says this about the Dead Zone where the Mississippi enters the Gulf of Mexico:

At 6,952 square miles, the size of these oxygen-deprived areas is determined by a number of factors, including nutrient discharge from fertilizer coming down the Mississippi River. The "long-term trend is still not changing," Don Scavia, an aquatic ecologist at the University of Michigan, said in a statement when the original prediction was released in June. "The bottom line is that we will never reach the dead zone reduction target of 1,900 square miles until more serious actions are taken to reduce the loss of Midwest fertilizers into the Mississippi River system."

The consequences of our modern industrial agriculture are multiple and devastating. A very concerning impact on the environment is the vanishing and extinction of many species. Insects are significantly affected by the frequent use of insecticides applied over immense surfaces. Reduced populations of honeybees and monarch butterflies are well documented. Massive extinction of insects is the earth's most severe known extinction event.

Another consequence of industrial agriculture is that the nations eating this way become overweight, weak, and partially intoxicated while living in a polluted environment. As we know, many illnesses such as diabetes and cardiovascular problems come directly from poor or unbalanced nutrition. Studies show a correlation between obesity (based on medical standards, over 60 percent of Americans are overweight) and a lack of essential nutrients in processed foods. Our brains do not trigger a feeling of satisfaction due to this lack of nutrients. Our spontaneous brain-body-gut feeling intelligence knows that there is still something essential missing and is asking for more. And the "more" is sadly often just more of the same: Big quantities of nutrient-depleted foods, mostly high in carbohydrates and fats.

When food is higher and more concentrated in essential nutrients, we eat less due to satiation, which is the end of our desire to eat during the meal. Nutrient-dense foods also produce more satiety, which increases the time-lapse between meals.

Processed foods are also packed with artificial flavors mimicking real nutrition, adding insult to injury. As a simple example, supermarkets will offer yogurt saying in big letters: Raspberry and Banana and then in small letters: *flavored*. The consumer sees the suggestion of fruit and has a taste of it even, but there is none of it!

The consumer is fooled, and sadly the producer is legally covered. There are very detailed and in-depth studies in the food industry on attracting and addicting people to processed foods, often by adding the precise artificial flavor or color.

We Americans like convenience. In a documentary, I recall hearing a foreign professor say: "The greatest fear of Americans is inconvenience."

Having grown up in another culture, I have to partially agree. The positive aspect of creating convenience is the desire to improve and facilitate life. Negatively, many conveniences seem attractive at first but serve only a minority of the society in the long run. This impacts the rest of us in an unfortunate and less obvious way. If the fear of inconvenience is triggered by a desire to avoid additional work, then sloth might have a lot to do with it. Everything has a price. Would we rather buy processed GMO potatoes with traces of glyphosate and other unknown and questionable additives ready for the microwave? Or do we prefer to peel and cook organic potatoes from the local farmer's market and know what we've got? It depends on what is important to us, but we don't have to be a fanatic about it. One does not have to exclude the other. We can prepare a healthy and responsible (organic) choice of potatoes quickly. We wash them, boil or steam them, or stick them in the microwave for a few minutes. Cut them in half; add some real butter, and some salt. If we don't feel like eating something that simple, skip a meal or two, and those potatoes will be the best thing we ever ate. A frequent comment about food from wise and enlightened people is: "Eat simply," which is also supportive of convenience.

Poorly Fed Soil Equals Poorly Fed Humans

As mentioned before, crops, orchards, and plants in industrial agriculture absorb the bulk of their nutrients from synthetic fertilizers. The soil becomes barely more than a physical support for plants fed "intravenously" and, therefore, must be "medicated" with pesticides. The soil becomes a dying body releasing carbon into the atmosphere. Consequently, it is in imperfect symbiosis with vegetation and microorganisms, as it was naturally and genetically programmed to be. The repercussion on animals, livestock, and humans is inevitable. Unfortunately, a significant majority of the Midwest, which was ironically some of the world's best soil, is managed industrially, producing predominantly corn and soy. Besides poverty in nutrients, there is poverty in variety. An article written in May 2019 from Susan Cosier in The Guardian, explains the problem simply:

>*"The world grows 95% of its food in the uppermost layer of soil, making topsoil one of the most important components of our food system. But thanks to conventional farming practices, nearly half of the most productive soil has disappeared in the world in the last 150 years.*
>
>*This threatens crop yields and contributes to nutrient pollution, dead zones, and erosion. In the U.S. alone, the cropland soil is eroding ten times faster than it can be replenished. If we continue to degrade the soil at the rate we are now, the world could run out of topsoil in about 60 years, according to Maria-Helena Semedo of the U.N.'s Food and Agriculture*

Organization. Without topsoil, the earth's ability to
filter water, absorb carbon, and feed people plunges.
Not only that, but the food we do grow probably be
lower in vital nutrients. The modern combination of
intensive tilling, lack of cover crops, synthetic ferti-
lizers, and pesticide use has left farmland stripped of
the nutrients, minerals, and microbes that support
healthy plant and soil life. But some farmers are at-
tempting to buck the trend and save their lands along
with their livelihoods."

Fortunately, to face this problem, many farmers have turned to no-till farming and the practice of cover crops in recent years. Cover crops, as the word says, are for soil conservation purposes. They do this by covering and protecting the soil instead of being a "cash crop." And indeed, an increase in organic matter is being observed. So far, so good, but overall, it remains a dilemma. The farmer is left with a choice between no-tilling and tilling, which necessitates much more herbicide and almost forces the use of GMO crops.

Soil conservation with minimum tilling and very minimal use of pesticides is a great art requiring many skills. It is, without question, more economical and efficient than industrial farming overall. The short-term huge yield crops supported by chemistry are mostly eye-catchers, short-term benefits for a few, and ruined landscapes and societies in the long run.

Many vegetables, tomatoes being a perfect example, are not grown in soil at all. The Netherlands, a tiny country, is the second biggest tomato producer in the world after Mexico! The Netherlands, in the northern latitudes, is not naturally suited to grow tomatoes. They are grown in greenhouses on fiberglass or rock wool instead. Producers add synthetic fertilizers in the drip irrigation systems. These fertilizers offer a much-reduced variety of nutrients compared to tomatoes in the soil, especially if organically grown. Consequently, the tomatoes lack nutrients, which is very noticeable in a total lack of flavor.

The production of synthetic fertilizers requires a lot of fuel. Consequently, the energy source of synthetically fertilized crops is primarily fossil fuel-based compared to organic fertilizing, which is solar-based. It is realistic to compare synthetic fertilizers for plants to processed food for humans. And if fed through an irrigation system, it becomes "intravenous" feeding, making crops grow big but weak. Everything is a matter of balance, and synthetic fertilizers are essentially not harmful or toxic in themselves. The problem is the enormous abuse and the miss-use of the soil. It becomes just a support for the plants and much less of a living element in symbiosis with them. Synthetic fertilizers should only be used sporadically to cover soil deficiencies or help build down excessive organic matter. However, it can quickly become a vicious cycle. That is because synthetic fertilizers themselves are what throws things out of balance and cause deficiencies. Well-established organic farms with livestock do not usually show any symptoms of imbalance in soil nutrients. As said before, the conventional massive overdose of synthetic fertilizers is the main reason for a lower percentage or concentration of nutrients in our food today. The concentration of nutrients can be remarkably lower, especially as crop varieties are selected to react well to synthetic fertilizers. Also, livestock feed has a lower percentage of TDN (Total Digestible Nutrients) and minerals when fertilizing synthetically. To visualize the problem, compare synthetic fertilizers to salt, and recognize that additional growth is mostly due to extra water.

So, it happens that we absorb fewer nutrients per meal. Still, the human stomach has remained the same size over the past millenniums. In the past fifty years, produce has lost 10–50 percent of its nutritional value.

A realistic comparison in a capitalistic society would be that of a wallet stuffed with one-dollar bills, which may not bring us through the day. But the same wallet full of bigger bills would!

Food Versus Nourishment

It is striking and interesting to note the choice of words we use in the English language, such as "food" and "feeding ourselves." How about the food industry! Doesn't that sound very close to "feed" and "commodity?" Unfortunately, very often, that's what it is. Yes, the word food comes from the United Kingdom originally. As much as I admire this country for many things, England is not known for its marvelous cuisine. I am convinced that food in England was undoubtedly simple and healthy before its industrialization. There is still excellent food or cuisine available if desired. But the choice of words shows the approach to it.

In comparison, Germans, for example, call food "Nahrung" or "Nahrungsmittel," which translates to nourishment or medium of nutrition. In French, it is called "aliments." There is no real translation for that in English. But the word "nourriture" is used, which also means nourishment. It is very common in America to say after eating that we are "full." This is almost shocking to other cultures. They would rather say, "I ate well" or "I am well served." Do you see a difference in the approach?

49

Variety and Concentration of Nutrients

We need to differentiate between the concentration and the variety of nutrients. The concentration tells us how many units there are in a serving. In contrast, the variety tells us how many types of nutrients are contained in one serving.

Based on analyses, 80–90 percent of the calories from a classic hamburger-fries and soda meal provided by fast-food chains are from corn and soy alone! Including the potatoes in the variety of nutrients, that makes three plants! Unfortunately, it is the same with most fast-food menus. Compare this to the same meal prepared with grass-fed/grass-finished mature beef, a multi-grain bun, and potatoes fried with peanut oil. You might choose a baked potato with real butter and sour cream from grass-fed cows instead, and a natural fruit juice. The nutrients in this meal are provided by several dozen plants instead!

Additionally, if grown organically, the concentration of nutrients is higher, up to 100 percent more, and toxin-free. When comparing these two dinners, the same menu, size, and basic look, we end up with very different nutritional values! It does not take a rocket scientist to find the healthier option.

Variety will allow us to have more flexibility and possibilities and bring us further through our day.

It is essential to realize that all things considered, the total cost of industrialized large-scale agriculture ends up being more expensive and more of a burden to the environment. We must include costs such as grain subsidies to farmers, extra fossil fuel energy, additional and oversized equipment, and other waste. Factor in the significant health issues due to fewer nutrients and toxicity from pesticides and pollution and the conclusion should be obvious. When we realize that we are also willing to pay a little more for our food. It is more cost-effective in terms of the environment and our health overall.

Concerning food awareness, it is also most important to mention the sad fact of enormous food waste in America today. Based on official statistics, we waste anywhere from 23 to 41 percent, depending on the calculation. Of course, zero-waste is not possible or realistic. Some waste is inevitable, but even the lower number of 23 percent is horrifically high. Food waste starts in the field and ends on the plate fueled by our ways of consumption. Growing up in Switzerland fifty years ago, throwing food away was an absolute no-no. Meals were reasonable portions, and we were required to finish our plates. The old saying in Switzerland: "The soup you serve yourself you finish!" sets the children's expectations. Food waste went to animals, from pets to chickens, pigs, or fish in ponds and streams. Many farmers picked up weekly food waste at restaurants or bakeries filled in old ten-gallon milk cans or large sacs.

What Happened?

The main change in how we produce and consume food in America happened on a large scale after the Second World War. What happened? There are many answers to that, depending on who you ask. We can analyze the technical, economic, political, and social approaches. We then realize that the problem manifests itself on all these levels as agriculture went from nourishment for societies to industrial food for the masses in a relatively short time. Instead, the root cause is human misbehavior in morality and responsibility on the journey of progress rather than any of the other issues mentioned before. Suppose technology has something to do with it. In that case, it is because technology rapidly outgrew us, and worst of all, we are not aware of it—more about that in the chapter Food for our Soul.

If we ask anybody around us about what went wrong with our food industry or other major issues, we will notice that the spontaneous and most common answer is that of Greed. That means our behavior's intention and direction is based on the thought process of "more for me and less for you," which is measured through finances. In other words, the focus is on the growth of personal profit. I recall a wealthy and successful CEO saying to my father: "If you want to understand how things work in this world, you must look at it through finances."

American culture has indoctrinated and brainwashed us over decades to put personal profit above all. It's all about personal gain. We have come to a point where we mix up democracy with capitalism. We perceive civic and social services as "socialism" while unconsciously and simultaneously benefiting from them. We think we are in a democracy and don't realize how much we resemble other forms of governance. Think about a plutocracy, which is a system regulated by a few, and an oligarchy, a system regulated by wealth. Personal profit is so highly revered that even gun-industry profits have apparent priority over our children's lives.

Violence is the tool used to gain additional territory, power, and control over others while abusing and destroying the environment. Lucid military service members are aware of this situation. "War is a racket," said Smedley Butler in his 1933 speech. He served in the military for decades. Further, he said, "I served in all commissioned ranks from Second Lieutenant to Major-General. And during that period, I spent most of my time being a high-class muscle-man for Big Business, Wall Street, and bankers. In short, I was a racketeer, a gangster for capitalism. I helped make Mexico safe for American oil interests in 1914. I helped make Haiti and Cuba a decent place for the National City Bank boys to collect revenues. I helped in the raping of half a dozen Central American republics for the benefit of Wall Street. The record of racketeering is long. I helped purify Nicaragua for the international banking house of Brown Brothers in 1909–1912. I brought light to the Dominican Republic for American sugar interests in 1916. In China, I helped to see to it that Standard Oil went its way unmolested. If only more of today's military personnel would realize that they are being used by the owning elite as a publicly subsidized capitalist goon squad, where only a few profit—and the many pay. But there is a way to stop it. You can't end it by disarmament conferences. You can't eliminate it by peace parleys at Geneva. Well-meaning but impractical groups can't wipe it out by resolutions. It can be smashed effectively only by taking the profit out of war."

This is a very particular and mostly unpopular point of view. At the same time, some of the countries where we intervened economically by force have profited overall. It is the worldly way that the stronger dominates and expands. The Greeks, Romans, Prussians, and French have done it, as have many others.

Of course, an enterprise has to be profitable or at least break-even to survive. The problem today is, and now more than ever, that there is too much emphasis on *personal* profit instead of win/win situations on a broader spectrum. The qualifier reduces to "what's in it for me financially, for my family, company, church, country?" instead of including the common good. The question should be what's in it for all of us? If it's not that, the approach remains on a purely material level and remains a never-ending power struggle. Today's corporate profits go mostly to their shareholders instead of recycled back into the company and into the primary workforce. How short-sighted!

Instead of providing nourishment for the society, the system turned into a food industry where the working class and laborers became part of the commodity. The military-industrial complex got progressively into motion about a century ago. The partially involved food industry started to suffer quality loss in the last half-century for the most part.

Today, conventional-industrial agricultural goods are generally judged by yields, appearance, and shelf life. At the same time, nutritional value and toxicity became secondary concerns. It is quantity over quality, which is financially beneficial to those who hold power. This approach cannot and will not go on for much longer because it is not sustainable for society or health. It is simply not economical and is too destructive.

On the positive side, we need a good military. It has helped many people make a living, no matter if directly or indirectly involved. Our military has helped the world twice in the past century, a world that would look much different today without our intervention. We countered the power of dictators and ruthless leaders and stood up for others. It has kept our country's freedom intact, something every generation has to fight for. Everything has a price, and we are undoubtedly grateful for everyone who has put so much into it.

On another positive note, more and more grass-root movements are coming up to defend nourishing and wholesome food. Many supermarkets now offer a choice of organic and sustainably raised food.

As a tree grows its roots deeper into the ground, at the same time, new branches reach out to the light!

Powerful Tools for Change

It is impossible to pinpoint the "bad guys" responsible for the deterioration of our food quality and the environment because we are all partially involved. From the ones pushing GMO grain for cattle in feedlots to the ones who snack on junk food without caring about the contents, we are all responsible. It is complicated to find the evildoers, which might be why it is called the industrial "complex." The more money someone controls, the more leverage they have. But as in the health system, there are also plenty of people of goodwill and good intentions working on every level of the industrial food industry. Our society got caught in a system, and people need work to live and survive. What would make the most significant difference is the right approach and good intention of every individual. It starts from the bottom to the top, from all the consumers to farmers, salespeople, engineers, feedlot operators, journalists, and CEOs. A change in attitude will result in proper and appropriate consumption and production.

Indeed, the top of the food industry hierarchy is more exposed and has more responsibility to show a good example. On the other hand, if the demand for healthy food grows, the market will adjust. We are all in it. We are all responsible for our current situation.

Whatever the activity, a person can influence the system either way: for selfish and personal interest or for all parties' benefit, including the environment. It is the direction, intention, and, finally, every individual's action, making the difference! Today, we are at a point where it becomes vital for our survival to take responsibility for our actions. We all have to contribute. So, it is critical what and how we consume. Most of us eat two to three times a day besides snacking. This represents enormous quantities of food and the energy to produce it. Therefore, our choices have about the most significant impact on our whole ecosystem. A change at the bottom will force a change at the top. The top will have to conform; the top depends on the bottom!

First and foremost is consciousness and then interest. Next, education will teach us to consume responsibly. Forks and knives are the most powerful voting tools for our economy!

Producing Responsibly

Fortunately, our food industry's deviation from healthy and natural standards is countered by a movement of conscious consumers and producers in many industrial countries. It is interesting to note that the demand for organic, locally sourced foods comes from coastal and populated areas or cities in America. Ironically, big grain farmers in the Midwest don't and can't eat anything of what they produce! How absurd! The shoemaker's children have no shoes! Today, most supermarkets, specialty stores, and farmers markets offer a choice of healthy foods. This is owing to conscious consumers, and the many farmers labeled organic or not, who produce naturally and locally. Many of these passionate and responsible farmers accept hard work, long days, and low pay. Many must have a job on the side to complete their income. In contrast, industrial grain farmers get help in the form of subsidies from the government, and they probably don't take a lot of pride in that. Profound contentment and the joy of producing quality foods have no price tag!

One of the pioneers and a popular farmer in this movement is Joel Salatin in Virginia. I highly recommend his books if you want to start to farm sustainably with livestock.

There is also a necessity for big farm or ranch operations, measured in sections rather than acres, to switch to a more organic model. Large operations are not necessarily in contradiction to sustainable agriculture. Natives were very efficient ranchers before Europeans killed all the bison. They managed huge herds, not just by hunting, but by consciously moving them to different territories. They were the first ranchers on this continent.

There is even space for the use of synthetic fertilizers and certain pesticides at times. But they should never be applied regularly and only in cases of strict necessity with the smallest amounts possible. Occasional applications of synthetic fertilizers to correct temporary nutrient deficiencies in the soil make sense. Still, they are not a replacement for natural organic plant food. Once the soils become healthy and living again, these corrections are not necessary anymore, as medications or food supplements are not essential for our health when eating nutritiously. Some fungal applications make sense to save a crop in jeopardy from mildew, for example. Minimal application is most likely less expensive in the long run, especially if including public health costs.

Production reflects the state of mind rooted in the spirit of the producer. To force a financially maximized cash crop with the help of many chemicals is fundamentally different than growing a crop from what the soil is ready to give with natural procedures. Organic farmers and their consumers are from a different spiritual family than industrial farmers and their bankers. The two may play golf together, but they don't mix well in the work field.

The Food and Health Industry

"People are fed by the food industry, which pays no attention to health and are treated by the health industry, which pays no attention to food."

-Wendell Berry

The food and health industry are *not* two separate things. The interest of a few in big corporations has forced the industrial complex onto agriculture, just like it has done in the medical field.

Over the time of my education and experience in agriculture, I have realized the chemical industry's impact on agriculture, their schools, and the farmers. Over the past few decades, corporations have gotten so out of hand in our society, in size and power, that they are dictating almost everything in education, science, media, politics, and law. The five most prominent mainstream media outlets are owned by corporations, powerful enough to buy and sell any information they want.

They are the "News," and they make the "News!" Let's not forget that. It is less about fake news than *not* saying what is going on and leaving the public ignorant. It is about prioritizing the information, which is beneficial to their sponsors. If NASA knew that a comet would strike the earth soon, there is a good chance that we would not be informed about it. Let's do our homework. Fortunately, it is possible to do today. Have you ever heard much about crop circles on the daily news? Were all the facts and conclusions of 9/11 presented to the public? And yes, there are also plenty of false conspiracy theories.

Who Has the Say?

When one single corporation is more powerful than some states put together, we know that democracy has had a serious blow. Sarcastically, shouldn't we add some stars on our beautiful flag to represent some of our most giant corporations or banks? They are more powerful and often have priority over individual states.

Mega corporations dictate behind the scenes to our federal and state governments. They certainly do so in schools and also impact many bureaucratic regulations. Regulation without representation is exactly what our forefathers wanted to avoid! This type of manipulation started to creep in mostly after the World War One and caused the depression ten years later. The situation turned around as the government's political leaders interfered and decided in favor of the working class. Unfortunately, and too often, it has to bleed before it leads. One of the impacting factors that led the government to interfere was that locals killed agents who went into the country to seize farms for foreclosure. President Franklin D. Roosevelt saw great danger. Consequently, he requested large sums of money from the most prominent industries at the time: steel, coal, and oil. He taxed them at a high rate for anything beyond a reasonable profit. With that and several other improvements in favor of the working class, he also created social security. America then entered the most robust era of its history.

The conscious push for mega-size farms in the Midwest started in the late seventies with Earl Butz, the Secretary of Agriculture under Presidents Nixon and Ford. He succeeded with strong sales arguments in favor of big industrial farming with enormous profits for just a few. Industrial agriculture pretends that increased production and yields were, and still are, to "feed the world" and to eradicate hunger in a rapidly growing population. Today, we see contrary results. Massive industrial farming destabilized the world farm economy. It led to nutrient depleted crops and soil, desertification, the burning of tropical forests for crops, etc. Industrial agriculture is the second biggest contributor to global warming and responsible for the loss of countless jobs. The reckless and relentless push for profit in the name of "freedom and democracy" and the worship of unlimited self-gratification turned our country into a plutocracy, a system regulated by a few, and an oligarchy, regulated by wealth.

Does democracy work in the long run? Churchill said that democracy is the worst way to run a country, but he did not know any better. So, what is the solution to return to healthy and sustainable agriculture?

Restriction for Freedom

Sports, especially martial arts and combat sports, show us parallels with life's inherent struggles well. Often, I tell my students from the youth program: "In Judo, the more you control yourself, the more options you have. It is the same in life; the more you restrict yourself, the more freedom you have." That is a challenging and unpopular lesson for our Western philosophy in general, especially for young people today. For example, suppose they want to have maximum energy for a competition. In that case, they need to restrict themselves from any smoking, drinking, overeating, partying, etc. If they want to drive their car, they need to restrict themselves to the speed limit and respect the rules of the road. Restriction is a bad word in our culture. Ironically, personal restriction leads to personal freedom and, ultimately, to more general freedom. Certainly, restrictions can be abusive when the elite in power impose them.

Still, society can choose to restrict corporations' power by proper and democratically voted resolutions as the forefather had planned and as it was until the early 1900s. No, that does not mean socialism or communism, where restrictions are imposed on the mostly working-class people by dictating elite. It is much more about a specific public consciousness and realizing the power of restriction applied to ourselves for the good of all. The only one we can change is ourselves. Together, we can change things in our family. A business owner can make drastic changes very quickly in his company. If we don't restrict or discipline ourselves as a person, group, company, or country, we actually lose freedom.

Interestingly, America has more restrictions on individuals and small businesses than we realize; we are just not aware of it. A few years ago, I met a man from the Ukraine living in Southern California for about five years. So, I asked him where he liked it better—in California or Ukraine. He answered that both were good places to live, both with their pros and cons, but what he preferred in Ukraine was more personal freedom.

Education

It is not only higher education that determines a country's level of functioning. General education or knowledge has a lot to do with the situation a country finds itself in. Sadly, when the leading forces become too powerful in a country, they are not interested in an educated society with awareness. They need the uneducated masses to execute their orders. Excellent higher education is still available in America for the ones who can afford it. But be aware that the level of general public education has dropped considerably in the past decades compared to other countries.

More awareness on a broad spectrum of the population would lead to improved consumption. It could transform and improve the working force's socio-economic and health systems. This transformation of our society would be beneficial to the environment in a relatively short time. At the same time, it would decrease the power of plutocracy, the current regime, as well. In other words, the middle class would grow again; low income and poverty diminish, and consequently, the abuse of power at the top would lessen. But that will not happen without crises.

Unfortunately, Covid-19 will probably not be enough to ignite that movement.

Proper education starts with parents being an example to their children. Working together and sharing daily meals as a family is a primary cornerstone. It is unnecessary to be a great chef to do home cooking. It is good enough to know how to cook a nutritious meal with whatever is around and without a cookbook. Children learn more than we are aware of by example, like watching parents cook or how they relate to each other. Parents have to be an example and teach discipline and self-control when it comes to food. Children should not have free access to the refrigerator or the cookie jar.

However, they should still have the opportunity of a healthy choice, like a fruit and nut basket. That is where it starts.

Growing up that way, we realize that we have a responsibility toward ourselves and the people around us because we do not live for ourselves alone!

Of course, we also need plenty of formal schooling. Much of the information through the internet is not regulated, out of respect for "free speech." Therefore, veracity remains an open question. A good example is an advertisement camouflaged as information. Dr. Andreas Novack, a renowned chemist in food science, states that over 90 percent of the information about food on the Internet is false or distorted. Here again, the reason for that is business self-interest or simply a lack of education.

Literature can be a great source of education. The book In Defense of Food written by Michael Pollan is probably one of the best books written to give us an essential and sufficient awareness of our current food industry in America. He very much opens our eyes to the situation and its consequences. A little more scientific and holistically oriented, Dr. Fred Provenza explains the loss of our society's relation and connection to our landscapes in his book "Nourishment." He describes the correlation, or lack of, science, culture, landscapes, and mythologies with exceptional knowledge and wisdom. Great books containing truth and wisdom never get old. Wendell Berry is another classic writer in this genre.

For all we read and study, it is essential to remain grounded. The best way to do this is to be hands-on, like growing and preparing our own food as much as we can. Farming, cooking, and life in general are mostly about doing. It is always good to follow sound advice, like the recommendation of the great naturalist and scientist Viktor Schauberger from Austria, who said to observe nature, understand nature, and copy nature.

Farmers have a great responsibility toward society and the environment. They can follow the advice of agro-chemists and their salesmen or decide to minimize their use of pesticide and synthetic fertilizers or switch to organic farming. Producers and providers of synthetic fertilizers and pesticides falsely believe that it is impossible to produce organically on a large scale nowadays because of hunger, worldwide population growth, and pests. Farmers like Gabe Brown, who operates on 5,000 acres in North Dakota, is proof that this belief is plain wrong and nonscientific. His soil and production are superior to his conventionally farming neighbors. It is actually the opposite. To be a sustainable, responsible, or organic farmer requires more homework, observation, personal decisions, and education.

Another major step to feed a growing world population would undoubtedly be to waste less. This is a big problem in the United States, as we waste almost one-third of our food supply. Reducing our meat consumption and entirely avoiding industrial meats and grain-fed ruminants would greatly contribute to a more efficient food supply. It would considerably reduce agricultural carbon emissions and reduce soil and water pollution! In Wikipedia, we find that worldwide, estimated food waste is around 1.3 billion tons per year, including 45 percent of all fruits and vegetables, 35 percent of fish and seafood, 30 percent of cereals, 20 percent of dairy products, and 20 percent of meat.

Hunger anywhere in the world is the result of power struggles, politics, and very recently of global warming, but certainly not as a result of yields! Many nonprofit-oriented economists say that large-scale industrial farming actually increases hunger and poverty through desertification, pollution, and vanishing species while seriously adding to climate change. The main source of these problems is the use or abuse of fossil fuels which we so utterly depend on today.

The Limitation of Growth

Our planet has a given size and is not growing. Therefore, and rationally thinking, the permanent growth of the economy that goes along with the world population growth is a grand illusion! The growth of world population is limited. A simple calculation tells us that the average calories necessary per person requires a minimum acreage of productive farmland in an area with sufficient precipitation or the possibility of irrigation. In the 1980s, scientists estimated that the maximum population capacity was about fourteen billion people based on the currently available farmland and current farm methods. Today, this capacity is estimated at around ten to eleven billion people. The world population in the year 2018 was 7.7 billion. It has been doubling about every forty years over a long period. This number includes the effects of wars and epidemics. Though, the growth curve flattened in the past years and is estimated to do so even more in the future. The doubling up is insignificant when the numbers are small but frightening when they get bigger. The following is a practical example that everyone can calculate. It illustrates the problem clearly: If we take a sheet of paper and fold it in half, we have two, next fold we have four, then eight, etc. How thick is our paper pile going to be if we keep doubling up the paper like this fifty times? Pause for a few seconds and try to estimate. For the ones not familiar with this calculation, here comes the shocker. The thickness of the pile would be half the distance from here to the sun! Not true? Within a couple of minutes, we have the proof by merely doing the calculation, starting with a sheet of paper of 0.1-mm thickness. Some countries are slow in their population growth, like Belgium, which has been doubling up approximately every 200 years until recently. But some African counties have been doubling up in ten years during that same time! Because the growth curve is getting flatter, we most likely will reach the full capacity of our globe in less than a few decades. To maintain the population at a steady rate, the average birth rate per woman should theoretically not be more than two children, starting today.

Whatever humanity will do or decide, these are the hardcore mathematical facts, and these numbers do not change; never have and never will. If we found a planet identical to earth, our new home would be at full capacity within less than a century without any changes in our expansion, way of life, and consumerism. So, what is the solution? The purely rational approach of limiting births would require enforcement, which is not acceptable for most nations and individuals. Will events that are out of our control provoke a large population reduction? No matter what, we are called to do our best and take responsibility as much as possible!

Isn't it said: "Help yourself, and Heaven will help you?" Philostro noted that the "human harvest" cycle, as he named it, is approximately every 7,000 years. He also said that no single spot of land on the planet remains more than 24,000 years without being covered by water or ice. We may accept this statement as a reality or go by purely scientific numbers. Still, we have an idea where humanity is heading.

As life is more about what we do than what we believe, let's move on, take responsibility, and start. An excellent first step is to eat and consume consciously and responsibly.

Diets

Many different diets have become popular in recent years, from vegetarian, vegan, paleo, macrobiotic, to low "carb," keto, etc. These are in addition to all individual and personal diets. In comparison, our ancestors generally ate what was put on the table and what was available and growing in their immediate area. They lived directly from their land and waterscapes and did not have many other choices most of the time. This scenario provided them with natural quality food.

Today, there is great confusion and misconceptions when it comes to diet. There are certainly several reasons for this, but globalization and facilitated food shipping are probably the primary reasons. Also, we have an overwhelming number of choices and a tsunami of information about food and diets everywhere. An obvious way to observe this confusion is to watch how we get lost in supermarkets trying to find the answer by reading the labels. It is very understandable how it got to that point because we have made it an immensely complex subject! Our ease of travel, media impact, and the proximity of many ethnic cultures combine to provide us with all the world's food types.

The connection to our landscapes or "terroir" got lost. Terroir is a French word that describes a territory or geographical area with its particular soil type, vegetation, topography, and local climate. It is a pearl of old wisdom and a concept that defines that, for many reasons, locally grown foods are the best for us. Philostro said that the necessary plants to cure our illnesses are growing right around our houses.

Nature is in constant evolution and subject to changes over time. Soil, microorganisms, plants, temperatures, and seasons continuously change, and therefore, our needs do also. All medications lose their effectiveness over time. Nutrition experts are much more challenged with all the processed and imported exotic foods. Therefore, diet advice becomes confusing and continuously modified. Medicine or health science comes up with opposite theories all the time. Margarine used to be better, and now it is butter again. Science deviates from the truth for commercial interest; nature does not. Margaret Floyd, a nutrition and dietetics specialist explains in a noncommercial and scientific way the difference between natural butter and margarine:

"Quality is paramount in dietary fats for several reasons. For one, the nutritional value of a quality fat is superior to a low-quality, refined, or modified version. Take butter that comes from a pastured cow. This butter contains conjugated linoleic acid (CLA), which has anti-cancer properties, helps prevent weight gain and stimulates muscle growth. This nutrient is virtually absent in cows fed grain or processed feed. Also, toxins tend to accumulate in fat. This means that if the animal has a high toxic burden from consuming pesticide-laden feed or has received high doses of antibiotics and a hormone, that toxic burden is going to be stored in its fat, which we will then eat."

The classic widespread theory of the "food pyramid for a healthy diet," which has been taught for decades in schools, is very questionable for good reasons. Just look at the high level of obesity, diabetes, and heart disease in America today. Nature evolves but remains wise and much steadier than the human eco-technical evolution. Therefore, nature remains the best basic guideline. Nature's intelligence beats human intellect anytime.

The U.S. Department of Agriculture sets nutritional guidelines for schools and the military. At the same time, it also represents corporate interests. It has a vested interest in promoting diets based on grain and meat, which have proven unhealthy in large quantities, especially with today's deterioration of quality.

Milk

For humans, milk is a nutritional foundation and one of nature's most perfect foods. I have an education in agriculture, specifically cattle husbandry, and dairy. I have milked and attended cows in Switzerland, France, and the United States. We will go a little more in-depth on this basic food topic. I hope to illustrate and raise more awareness of some of the problems in our food chain today.

Today's industrial milk in the United States is barely comparable to milk from natural grassy land-scapes in America decades ago. Fortunately, there are still responsible dairy operations, which go out of their way to produce naturally. Many countries have centuries, if not millenniums of experience with dairy. They have proven that milk from herbivores is an excellent nutrition source, consumed as such, or processed into cheese, butter, or cream.

Our culture understands the concept of quality very well when it comes to automobiles. We are ready to pay the price for superior convenience and performance. However, many are not aware of differences in quality regarding essential foods such as produce, dairy, meat, or eggs. In general, we don't give it much thought. Why is this, when it considerably impacts our health, our society, the environment, and ultimately the whole socio-economic system? Is it because of the inconvenience of thinking about it, or is it the mistrust of our intuition? Is it the complexity of the topic or naïve trust in the regulatory system? Most likely, it is a little bit of all of that. Unfortunately, even some medical doctors will say that basically, an egg is an egg or milk is milk. How ignorant!

Nutritionally, there is no comparison between conventional industrial milk from the supermarket and organic milk from cows grazing on local natural pastures, hills, and mountain slopes as it used to be. These cows are feeding freely and choosing from dozens or even hundreds of different plants, grown without the addition of synthetic fertilizers and pesticides. The cows are free of antibiotics and hormones. The milk is coming from cows with balanced genetics adapted to the environment. They are therefore producing reasonable amounts of milk. This milk is often consumed whole and not pasteurized or is processed into cheese or any other dairy product within less than twenty-four hours.

Increasing lactose intolerance is a symptom and proof of a natural reaction to commercial industrial milk, mostly due to pasteurization. Margaret Floyd explains why: "Milk pasteurization damages the delicate enzyme lactase, which is required to digest the milk sugar lactose. As babies, all of us produce lactase. That's how we're able to digest breast milk. But in some people, lactase production declines massively by around age four, when, being fully weaned, we would have no more need for it. When drinking raw milk, this doesn't pose a problem: the milk comes with its own lactase to digest the lactose. The problem occurs when drinking pasteurized milk. Having no lactase in either the milk or the person drinking it leads to digestive distress and diarrhea, a condition called lactose intolerance. And yet, many people who are lactose intolerant not only tolerate raw milk but thrive on it."

If we observe nature and copy nature as much as possible, we can't go wrong. Naturally, milk goes from breast to mouth without being exposed to light, and it is supposed to be for babies. A series of studies have found no evidence that cow milk itself improves bone health for adults. The milk myth has been abused and pushed by the dairy industry, which lobbies the USDA. Pasteurizing milk is certainly not nature's way! It only fixes some problems caused by mismanagement of cows and milk. It also eliminates liability issues for the dairy industry.

You may read on the internet: "Raw milk is milk that hasn't been pasteurized or heated to kill bacteria. It goes straight from the cow to your table. Skipping the pasteurization step means that the same bacteria that can be found in beef may also turn up in your daily glass of calcium: Salmonella, Campylobacter, and E. coli."

It is undoubtedly true and vital to know that these harmful parasites can develop and cause serious health problems or even death. It is only so if milk and livestock are handled unprofessionally and with a lack of care. Europe's alpine areas have been producing raw milk cheese for centuries and still do it successfully and safely. Pasteurizing is useful and necessary for mass production when shipping long distances, storing for extended times, and during outbreaks of specific parasites. It is also a guarantee to avoid irresponsible and careless milk management by some farmers or processors. The necessity for pasteurization is additionally related to the "liability culture" in this country. The Minister of Agriculture recently stated, "The human race existed long before Louis Pasteur was heard of." Most dairy farmer families drink raw milk and have no problem. It is true that pasteurizing milk simplifies the work process, eliminates just about all risk of pathogens, and increases shelf life considerably. Simultaneously, it certainly results in a mediocre product eliminating many of the good benefits.

For these reasons, milk is the best example. Our food should not be shipped over long distances losing freshness, but rather produced and consumed as locally as possible.

There are experienced Swiss dairy farmers who produce cheese with raw, organic, and alpine grazed milk. They know their small herd of cows so well that they can tell by tasting which cow produced the milk and specifically in which area they have been grazing. I have personally experienced, seen, and worked with this kind of production, and believe me; you can feel the power in that kind of milk and cheese! It is alive! It is a day and night comparison to dead, industrialized-pasteurized, diluted, and intoxicated commodity milk, which is commonly found in supermarkets. It is offered at extremely low prices but ends up more costly overall considering the loss of health benefit. These costs start with hidden farm subsidies for grain production for livestock and end with expensive health issues for the consumer.

Industrial milk comes from overfed cows fed with mostly three to four different plants, like corn and soy, corn silage, and alfalfa, all GMO feed treated with glyphosates. The feed is often shipped over long distances. Cows are concentrated together and breathing ammonia saturated air. Dairy cows are genetically over bred with a production capacity four times or more over their natural state (the need of the calf). They are bred from a very narrow and uniform gene pool, mostly Holstein, geared for high volume production. Milk production is enhanced with daily applications of synthetic hormones and the overuse of antibiotics because of frequent mastitis (an infection of the udder mostly due to overproduction and large amounts of grain causing a cow's weaker health). Milk is bleached and highly pasteurized; several days if not weeks old; "low fat" because it is stripped of cream. . . All in all, an insane product! Health-conscious people have indeed the right to say that regular consumption of (industrial) dairy should be avoided! There was no question about the many benefits of dairy products and no health issues before milk's industrialization. Got *good* milk?

There are some responsible producers, fortunately, who are making a great effort to deliver a much better product. It is now possible to find whole and organic milk in most supermarkets. Some stores even sell raw milk and raw milk dairy products. There are also outstanding cheese makers in this country. We can show our gratitude and honor these people by buying their products while doing something good for our health. We are supporting sustainable farming and responsible animal husbandry. Of course, it remains personal if dairy products suit us, but it certainly has a lot to do with the quality. It is no coincidence that dairy products raise health concerns today because they are no longer the same products.

Advanced technology is not in contradiction to the natural, but the closer we get to natural, the better. It's as simple as that!

Besides Nutrients

Besides nutrients and the chemical composition of food there is another lesser-known aspect of quality. It is a form of energy that is very difficult to measure within the current traditional scientific procedures. Physicists and naturalists have worked on devices to measure these forms of energy. However, it is still not consistently quantifiable or scientifically measurable. It seems like this energy is almost too "fluid" to measure.

Simply said, this form of energy appears at first glance to be something like a form or sub-form of electromagnetic energy, but it is neither. Vitality might be the closest popular word used in everyday language. This energy is interconnected in all living beings in good health and, therefore, also in good food. The Hindus may call this form of energy prana, which means nothing else than "life" or "life energy." Wilhelm Reich was probably one of the scientists able to measure, reproduce, and concentrate a type of this energy in the 1940s, which he named Orgone. The following explanation can be found on the Internet:

"Orgone Energy is another name for healthy or beneficial negative Ions. These are found in Nature not disturbed by human-made influences, such as around waterfalls, mountains, and the sea. Orgone Energy means the energy frequency of Nature."

When two physically similar people, maybe even twins, with similar lifestyles and diet go on a strenuous hike, why does one tire much more quickly than the other? Why was it possible hundreds of years ago to obtain from large groups of people (soldiers) performances far beyond what similar groups of people can accomplish today?

Dowsers have developed a natural trait to sense these kinds of energies. Experienced dowsers say that most people have this sensitivity or capacity but that it must be developed. Dowsing is not understood, and traditional science is very critical of it. Using the word dowsing in a strictly rational scientific environment is equivalent to cussing in church. But it is interesting to note that many people, when locating a spot to dig their well, want the opinion of a dowser or "water witch." Dowsers can also detect negative zones, which can cause insomnia or inexplicable aches and pains.

The most complete and balanced nutrition for new-borns is mother's milk. It is meant to go directly from breast to mouth and usually within the same species. Milk should neither be exposed to light nor stored at any time; it is naturally and genetically programmed that way. That is the reason unprocessed milk has a minimal shelf life and does not keep. Every living thing from bacteria to mammals likes milk, but it goes "bad" very quickly. Compare this to seeds or grains, which have an excellent preservation potential and can still germinate after years or even decades. Milk has no "life span" once it has left a warm body. If not processed within hours, milk cannot store or keep its vitality, the energy form explained above. In its concept, it is not meant to do that. Dowsers who have the gift to feel the intensity of this vital energy say that milk loses a considerable amount of it within only one hour and about all of it within twenty-four hours. If you have the opportunity to enjoy milk coming straight from the milking bucket or milk tank from grazing cows, still warm, you should try it! It feels better on the stomach, before, during, and after consuming it than any commercial milk. It will also raise your vitality level, especially if the cow is strong and healthy, and will not make you tired and sleepy. If you pay attention, you can feel that.

Based on the perception of people who can feel this energy, foods relatively high in vitality are, for example, seeds, nuts, or virgin cold-pressed olive oil. Fresh picked ripe fruits and vegetables are a good source as well. Consequently, many processed and canned foods are almost exempt from this vital energy and can be considered "dead." While organic foods free of toxins are a step forward, they won't have much life left in them if they are highly processed.

An Aspect of Food Choices

We cannot totally grasp the subject of diet. It is a living and continuously changing thing because life is in permanent motion. This is one reason why highly evolved spirits hardly ever talk about food. Their example and their comments usually focus on eating simply, and that says a lot!

We also all have different metabolisms and different activities. Therefore, everyone has to find the type of diet that suits them best. We need to pay attention to our own bodies' natural requests for nourishment. We trust our intuition or "inner knower," rather than being distracted by diet recommendations, food labels, and fashions.

Overeating is a strong tendency in industrial societies. Not only is food so cheaply and readily available everywhere, but most processed foods also have little or no vitality. They do not trigger satiety or satiation anymore. Discipline in the quantity of food intake is another subject that remains a personal issue. We will look at it in the following chapter under "Food for Our Soul."

A healthy and straightforward suggestion for Americans would be to consider Michael Pollan's recommendation in these simple seven words: Eat food, not too much, mostly plants. He also says, Eat and cook like your grandmothers, which would most likely be great-grandmothers for the younger generation of today.

To know about and pay attention to longstanding cultural traditions is a good indicator of a healthy and sustainable food source. It is also wise to observe what people were thriving on over long periods within their nearest landscapes and see which foods passed the test of time.

Simultaneously, we need to remember that everything changes and evolves, which requires modifications to our eating habits. Produce and farm goods have changed or been modified over time, either through natural adaptation, selection or genetic modification. The changing environment impacts natural genetic modification of plants and animals even without human intervention. It is the slowest process. Humans have naturally selected the healthier and more performant plants and animals to their advantage since agriculture has existed. The human impact of simple selection accelerates the process of modification considerably. Today, with genetically modified plants and organisms, we take shortcuts, instantly and directly impacting the organism's genetic growing program. As we all know, this process is debated vigorously. We must realize that genetic modification has not passed the test of time. Short-term experiments on rats are not sufficient and not transparent. Natural selection reflects the choice of Mother Nature. The selection created by humans through agriculture usually serves the whole society. GMOs are only in the financial interest of a few.

On our farm, we avoid GMOs by all means, and for several reasons. We do not trust the product; neither do we trust the commercial-interest oriented science behind it, which says that it is safe. Nonprofit-oriented scientists like Dr. Jeffrey Smith warn against consumption of GMO's. Last and most convincing, is that we observed that deer on our property prefer by far non-GMO alfalfa pellets over the GMO type. Many farmers have observed the same with their livestock. These are not personal opinions! Another interesting observation is that our cats devour our beef livers (grass fed and organic) and only eat liver from commercial beef if very hungry. We do not know if it is because of the GMO grains, which were fed to these commercial feedlot cattle, because of antibiotic residues, or something else.

Crop selection has benefits but can be misguided depending on its purpose. For example, to facilitate industrial bread-making, wheat has been over-selected in the past decades to obtain higher gluten content. Consequently, and in addition to other factors, bread, which has been a healthy and primary food source over thousands of years, suddenly raises health concerns. The same old-fashioned bread recipe will make something different today than in the past.

It was not that long ago no grains or salmon were genetically modified. Ruminants were not fed with grain. And oils were not solidified to obtain dangerous trans fats and fake butter. For many reasons, going back to the old and natural ways would benefit the whole society and environment. Our most basic foods would be healthier again.

Diet and Activity

As we all know, our type of activity impacts our diet considerably. Still, we must be careful not to over-intellectualize our food choices. That is not necessary; our body will usually tell us what food we need and how much of it. We need to pay attention to our gut-feeling and avoid numbing it out. The only thing we need our brains for concerning nutrition is to discern between natural and living food versus highly pro-cessed food. Here again, Michael Pollan's sound recom-mendation is simple and easy to remember: "As a general rule, do not buy or consume food which has more than five ingredients."

It is undoubtedly best to stick as far as possible to single foods without any ingredient label, like produce, grains, plain meats and fish, oils, spices, etc. Basic healthy foods like that are all we need. Remember that there are no ingredients listed on a crate of raspberries, which have approximately 2,000 different natural nutri-ents, based on the German chemist Dr. Andreas Noack.

If we want to know what we are really eating, it is the best to assemble basic ingredients and cook for ourselves as much as possible. We will then spontaneously understand what we need and redefine this body intelligence. Our body is not being told lies with artificial flavoring and colors anymore. Is it inconvenient? If we include the time, cost, and unnecessary and inconvenient health consequences, maybe less than we think.

Everything has a price, but once people discover the joy of preparing their food, they do not go back to regularly buying pre-packaged meals. It is better to decide to make an effort first and be ahead of the game instead of being enslaved by health issues.

Ideally, everyone would grow some of their food. For most states, and if appropriately managed, a spot of fifteen by thirty feet would be sufficient to produce a large part of the vegetables a person needs per year.

It is easy to understand that a small hybrid car requires much less and different fuel than a big construction vehicle or truck. Similarly, a musician or computer technician's activity requires different types and amounts of food than someone peeling logs or racing in the Tour de France. But again, there is no need to overthink our needs if our consumption relies on natural ingredients. Our intuition knows better and will tell us.

Simply Water

Certain health recommendations have indoctrinated the masses by repetition over many years and have highjacked our common sense. It is a general and broad medical recommendation that we should drink eight glasses of water per day. Are we all doing this? Is this a need in all circumstances and for every adult? The answer is yes and no. Our need for water depends tremendously on physical activity, size, quantity and quality of our food, and the climate. The numbers mentioned above are indicated for average people and situations. While it is correct that the average person needs approximately seventy ounces (half gallon) of water every day, it is false that this volume is necessary every day in addition to other liquid intakes. One or two generations ago, no one walked around with a bottle of water. No one said they were dehydrated; instead, our bodies told us when we were thirsty, and we drank water from the faucet or the fountain between or during meals. People got to be old before and were as healthy or healthier than today. My father can still run to the bus stop at ninety years of age if he has to. I hardly ever saw him drink water between meals unless working in the garden on hot days. The eight glasses of water per day recommendation is questionable since our need can vary from no additional water to two gals/day thirty-two glasses!), depending on our activity. As most of our society works in air-conditioned spaces, the amount of water needed is lower. No need to intellectualize our need for water; the body knows better. Keep in mind that the number indicated by science is not wrong but includes the water contained in our food! Soup, tea, coffee, fruit juice, or milk is mostly water. Most fresh produce contains approximately 85 to 95 percent water. Even meat, fish, eggs, and cheese contain about 80 percent water.

Companies selling bottled water were happy to go hand in hand with general medical advice. They pushed us to "think" that we have to drink a lot of their water every day. From their perspective, there is no liability in advocating for increased water consumption and no apparent risk in the short term. Who would think that drinking a lot of water can be negative? It can. Drinking too much water can also be harmful. The amount of salt and other electrolytes in your body can become too diluted. Hyponatremia is a condition in which levels of sodium (salt) and other electrolytes become dangerously low. Consequently, Gatorade got into the business of selling water with electrolytes typically found in all healthy essential foods.

Bottled water became a huge business in these past years. Simultaneously, our modern diet of overeating, consuming too much salt, sugar, caffeine, and toxins does indeed require us to drink sufficient water.

As usual, thinking for ourselves and mostly following our intuition helps us to drink the right amount. Animals usually do not eat and drink at the same time, and they drink cold water slowly. Americans often consume large quantities of ice-cold water or sodas with their meals, something no other culture in the world does. It is debatable if cooling down greasy food with ice-cold drinks causes health issues. Indeed, ice-cold water and sweet sodas with a meal numb down our digestion, and the next thing needed is caffeine from Starbucks. Many older cultures drink hot tea with their meals.

Shipping bottled water worldwide is one of the biggest offenders for our carbon footprint or wasting fossil fuel energy. Water is heavy and requires a lot of energy to ship, while it is normally available in every household. Burning fuel to ship or fly water nationwide or worldwide is one of our current biggest economic nonsenses. It is an excellent example of the unnatural and dysfunctional behavior of Homo sapiens today. Unfortunately, and as we all know, some of our public water is contaminated. This contamination can be from lead pipes like in Flint, Michigan, or nitrates in Iowa caused by industrial agriculture. In these cases, tap water can be purified with an active carbon filter to remove lead.

Activated carbon filters will also remove other impurities but unfortunately, not nitrates, which require a system with reverse osmosis. Eliminating toxins is undoubtedly a significant first step, but it is also best to revitalize this water. Johann Grander from Austria, a naturalist who developed water revitalizing devices, explains that water has memory. Toxic water that has been purified still contains the memory of intoxication. The system he developed offers a method to revitalize water back to its natural state. There are other proven methods to improve water life, for example, treatment with magnets.

By the way, repeatedly reusing the same water bottle will also reduce pollution, carbon in the air, and plastic in the ocean. Suppose you are not sure about the quality of your tap water. In that case, cities and towns are obligated to provide water analysis results by law. Still, it is the best to have your water analyzed by a private lab exempt from local political or economic influence.

Eating Meat or Not?

Of the many different types of diets followed and practiced today, vegetarianism is probably the most common. Avoiding all animal-based proteins as vegans do is more restrictive. It requires much more discipline and ideology and is, therefore, less popular. Based on studies, for example, by Wolf-Dieter Storl, there have been no cultures throughout history that have been strictly vegetarian. Based on his research, the first broader vegetarian movement started in India's recent past due to excessive numbers of cattle slaughtered as offerings to the gods. Science tells us that humans have always been and still are omnivores. Healthy or not, ethical or not, we have to decide for ourselves. What about the Eskimos and other arctic tribes who work hard physically outdoors in the cold, fish, and hunt in the polar zone? There is nothing better than their traditional diet consisting almost entirely of fish and meat. The first Europeans who pioneered in Alaska's arctic zones became ill if they did not eat sufficient animal fat. These fats are essential in the far northern climate. They are naturally high in omega-three fatty acids, vitamin K1 and vitamin D3, which originate from greens, either from the ocean floor or from land, but not from agricultural grains. People living in the northern United States and Canada endure short, cold winter days with little sun exposure and also depend on sufficient animal fat. In his book, Nourishment, Dr. Fred Provenza reviewed evidence that on average, one bite out of three from fish or meat should be fats originating from herbivores eating diverse species of plants. He explains: "During the nineteenth-century, explorers of the Canadian arctic who were forced to live only on the lean meat of wild rabbits experienced a condition called rabbit starvation. No matter how much they gorged on rabbit, they were unremittingly hungry. After just seven days, explorers were eating three to four times more rabbit than at the beginning of the week, and by day ten the swelling of their distended bellies was visible through layers of clothing. When they ate only lean meat, they became ravenous for fat. They were attempting to eat enough fat, present only in low amounts in rabbit, by over-eating rabbit. Given a chance, they'd eat a large quantity of pure fat, even oily fat, without nausea. Without fat, they died in a few weeks." Rabbits were a common meat source in their native France and were plentiful in their new hunting grounds, but not suited to their current diet that lacked fat.

In contrast, a person with little physical activity living in a moderate or warm climate zone offering a wide variety of produce, grains, and nuts can survive very well on a vegetarian diet. Their reduced need for essential animal fats can be met with dairy and eggs. Vegetarians usually remain very healthy or, on average healthier throughout their lives than the average citizen who abuses meat consumption in the same geographical situation. It is a fact, people and countries with a predominantly plant-based diet live longer. Heavy meat eaters have a naturally shorter life span, usually related to a rougher environment and lifestyle that requires that diet.

Over the past years, the Mediterranean Diet has been called the healthiest one. Yes, certainly for people living in the Mediterranean area or a similar habitat, but not for people in much colder climates. All latitudes and altitudes have their specific vegetation and forms of life. These will naturally provide the traditional foods adapted to the people of that area. Agriculture also adapts to these conditions. For example, oats and rye are the northern grains, wheat and barley from intermediate latitudes, and rice and corn from the southern latitudes.

Meat and Physical Performance

Those who assume that meat consumption is indispensable for top physical performance should be aware of people like Paavo Nurmi. He was a Finnish middle and long-distance runner at the turn of the century who won several Olympic gold medals and was a vegetarian. He had this to say: "All that I am, I am because of my mind. Muscles are pieces of rubber." The author Dan Millman, a world-class gymnast, a sport that requires powerful and strong muscles, has been a vegetarian throughout his sports career and up to this day. On the other hand, the Russian weightlifter Vasily Alekseyev who was considered the strongest man in the world in the 1970s, consumed enormous amounts of eggs, milk, cheese, and meat daily. On the morning of his Olympic medal performance in Montreal, he ate twenty-six fried eggs and a steak for breakfast. One night after another record, he ate a whole lamb leg by himself. He died at age sixty-nine of heart failure. Gary Null, a New York scientist, activist and athlete has been a vegan all his life. He did body building in his younger years winning local tournaments and still runs marathons past retirement age to this very day.

To conclude, the choice of a plant versus animal diet on a purely medical scientific approach seems to boil down to the following: "Most humans are omnivores who satisfy their needs for nourishment with a combination of animal and plant foods. While differences among individuals in form and function help to explain why some people can thrive on either animal- or plant-based diets (Williams, 1988), most people can best meet their needs with a combination of meat and plants. Animal and plant foods thus function symbiotically to nurture human health" (reviewed in van Vliet et al., 2020ab).

An Ethical Approach to
Meat Consumption

Vegetarians and especially vegans also have an ethical approach to their choice of diet besides health reasons. These are very necessary and important actions and reactions in a world of industrial meat mass production and intolerable animal abuse.

It is, among other reasons, a respectful act and an effort of vegetarians or vegans to object to cruel industrial meat production. Even as a farmer with cows myself, I strongly believe it is better for the well-being of all life forms to be vegetarian or vegan than to consume industrial animal products. To be a vegetarian or vegan requires consciously or unconsciously a genuine effort for most. Neurological tests on these people show, and this is true among the ones saying or pretending they can't eat meat anymore, that the brain continues to send strong signals of craving for animal protein and fats. To be a vegetarian or vegan is an admirable discipline of the spirit over the body.

Mahatma Gandhi, one of the great nonviolent activists in human history, was a leader in this way. He once said to his doctor when he had pleurisy: "I will not take milk, milk products or meat. If not taking these things should mean my death, I feel I'd rather face it." When faced with another health issue later in life, he finally gave in to drinking goat's milk. He would never consume cow or buffalo dairy products because of the abusive practice of phooka, also called cow blowing, a cruel method to increase milk production then practiced in several cultures.

In contrast, Adolf Hitler was a vegetarian during the Second World War, from 1937 to the end of his life in April 1945. However, he would occasionally eat some liver dumplings, bratwurst, or ham. A woman who was his food tester said once that she had not seen any fish or meat over a period of two years.

The Dalai Lama, one of the most ethical and compassionate souls known to us in current times, eats meat about twice a week. He was a vegetarian for almost two years. But he started eating some meat for health reasons and on his doctor's advice after developing gall bladder issues and hepatitis.

Philostro also ate meat on occasion, though he said humans were originally not meant to eat meat. He also said that we should not eat wild birds because they are not meant to be consumed, and as little game as possible. We should not eat the hearts or brains of animals, as there is "too much of the animal in it," he explained.

Some esoteric movement ideas say that ethnic groups like Eskimos are functioning on a "low frequency" or "vibration." Are they sure of that? How much experience do these people have living with Eskimos? Simple living people are certainly as good as sophisticated societies within any other culture. Eskimos, Bushmen, or aborigines have their spiritual leaders or shamans who lead their communities, heal their sick, and communicate with the spirits. Eskimos have their way to communicate with spirits, who will lead them to the best fishing grounds hidden under the vast ice surfaces. Some might say that these people are dealing with evil forces. Really? Evil forces who served them kindly over thousands of years?

What about those who have an almost effortless and comfortable physical life, and who, out of ignorance or lack of compassion, eat industrial meat three times a day? Isn't it real evil to willfully ignore the tremendous suffering of factory animals, while at the same time, some pets are treated like gods?

Opinions and ways of life are based on our education but can also come from indoctrinated beliefs. That is why we have to live according to our consciousness and find ways to live, love, observe, think and decide outside the box or out of common worldly ways. Most of the time, we avoid that because we don't want to take any risk and avoid exposing ourselves to unknown territory.

As a part-time farmer producing and selling grass-fed and grass-finished beef, I absolutely respect vegetarians and fully support people who refuse to buy and consume conventional and industrial meat, dairy products, or eggs. I do the same.

We raise our cattle using our best conscious effort in the most suitable environment and condition possible. Our mature steers are roaming eleven months per year on free range in pastures and forests. They were nursed by their mother for at least eight months, had no grain, no medications, no antibiotics, and no hormones. To avoid stress, we do no brand or castrate. Instead, ear tags and sterilizing rubber bands are put on in their first week of life. When they have reached full maturity at about thirty months, the trip to a small local butcher is only one hour away. It is made with a trailer providing plenty of space. The steers do not seem to be stressed by any means, but we do not know if they ignore what is going on. When delivering the steers, I pray for them and thank them for their lives, and I let them know that we don't want to harm them. I tell them that they are more than welcome to come back within our next calf crop the following spring. We are always sad to see them go. In the beginning, I used to assist the killing of our steers and helped to butcher them. As it was a small family-run butcher shop, the animal was led calmly into a parlor. The steers hardly ever seemed nervous. A special gun is held to the head, and a pin of approximately four to five inches in length shoots into the brain, which knocks them out instantly. Unconscious, the steer is immediately bled by cutting the throat artery. I love animals and do not have the heart to hunt, yet I can take responsibility for everything we do with our cattle.

Producing dairy inevitably will create a lot of animals not destined to become cows. Also, cows need to be replaced as they get old. What else to do with these animals is a legitimate question to vegetarians. Is it better to let them die of old age, which may involve suffering? If so, the price of dairy would probably be about three times as high. Vegetarians must be aware that they are automatically responsible for a certain amount of meat with dairy and egg consumption, whether they eat the meat or not. Americans consume an average of 275 lbs. of dairy per year, which includes 200 lbs. of fluid milk. Based on a calculation, that makes the average consumer (which includes vegetarians) automatically responsible for a minimum of 12 lbs. of beef per year. This breaks down to almost four ounces per week or two hamburgers per month. A total commitment to avoid killing any animals also requires eliminating any leather or wool. Some people do that, but how far does our responsibility go? While it is a fact that the average American overeats meat, it is also a fact that physical life consists of consuming other living beings. Consume and be consumed. For one species to live, another has to die. Humans are at the top of the food chain and are only consumed by other species once dead. In normal circumstances, we are not consumed by other species while alive. Still, we reduce each other through finances and decimate each other through wars.

Our physical exterior looks are all relatively similar. Still, our spirits and souls can vary enormously from one person to the other. Everyone has to find out what type of nutrition is suitable for their whole being because food also feeds our soul.

As a rule of thumb, it is good to adjust our fuel naturally to our needs. Needs based on our physiological type, activity, environment, the season of the year, and the zone or climate we live in, just as our ancestors naturally did. Typically, this would happen without any conscious management if we were more connected to our natural and local food sources. As Dr. Fred Provenza says, our society has lost the link to the soil and our landscapes.

"Palates link animals with foodscapes—those parts of landscapes animals including humans use to nourish and self-medicate—through three interrelated processes. First, all creatures must have access to a variety of wholesome foods. The more they are restricted—for instance to a feedlot ration for livestock or ultra-processed foods for people—the less they can sustain health. Second, mother is a transgenerational link to foodscapes. Her knowledge—of what and what not to eat and where and where not to go to forage—is essential for helping her offspring get a start in life. Her influence begins in the womb (through flavors in her amniotic fluid) and continues at birth (through flavors in her milk) and when her offspring begin to forage (as a model for what and what not to eat). Third, liking for food is mediated by feedback from cells and organ systems, including the microbiome, in response to nutritional and medicinal needs that are met by nutrients (energy, protein, minerals, vitamins) and the thousands of compounds plants produce (phenols, terpenes, alkaloids)."

The aim and idea of consuming natural and local foods should not be only to live longer, but to live responsibly toward all and to live well with energy and joy. At the same time, it eliminates unsustainable and partially intoxicated food production and animal factories.

On our little farm, we grow our yearly need for vegetables, bulbs, fruits, and herbs. Meat is from our grass-fed beef, eggs from our chickens that run around wherever they want. We occasionally catch fish from nearby streams or lakes, although most fish (wild-caught, not farmed) is purchased. If possible, we buy other necessities from organic and local sources. We restrict our meat consumption to about two to three times per week, a little more in the winter months, and less in the summer. Meat, particularly red meat, will heat up the body temperature, which is unnecessary and undesirable in the hot summer months.

A lady once said to me, jokingly: "You will die very healthy." Unfortunately, she missed the point. This nice lady died as a middle-aged heavy smoker from a sudden and fatal heart attack.

Manufacturing Diseases with Animal Factories

Many believe that the factory production of animals (CAFOs = Concentrated Animal Feeding Operations) could be a significant cause of cancer. It is certainly a source of several known diseases, for example, bird flu, swine flu, and mad cow disease. COVID-19 may have originated and spread in Wuhan, China's major meat and fish markets, and developed very rapidly in our country's meatpacking plants.

Conventional beef from feedlots with a high concentration of cattle, like Harris Ranch in Central California, cover 30 percent of the state's beef consumption! Before feeder cattle enter feedlot operations at approximately eight to nine months, they first get several vaccines. Bovine respiratory disease is the primary cause of cattle death in feedlots. They are fed a low fiber concentrate containing 75 to 85 percent GMO grains, mostly corn, grain side products, soy, and a small addition of GMO alfalfa. Cattle are naturally ruminants and are not meant to feed on grain. Consequently, they receive "approved" antibiotics (bacitracin, chlortetracycline, oxytetracycline, tylosin, and virginiamycin) to avoid liver abscesses due to heavy grain feeding. Most cattle would not survive this diet without antibiotics and have no other choice than to feed on this minimal selection of three to four grains and one green. Grass-fed cattle would instead be choosing freely among dozens of different grasses and legumes on pastures. Also, steers usually receive growth hormones, which are very questionable concerning their effects on human health. Whatever the FDA (Food and Drug Administration) approves and guarantees as safe is for the short term but not for the long run.

For profitability, feeder cattle get butchered prematurely at sixteen to eighteen months. After that age, the curve of the growth/feed ratio starts to flatten. It takes typically thirty-six months for cattle to fully mature and for the muscles (meat) to be supplied with all necessary nutrients. Industrial food production commonly prioritizes short-term financial profit over nutritional values and long-term benefits.

Unfortunately, other animal production methods are no better and are rather worse, as most of these animals never see sunlight! At least beef cattle enjoy a decent and healthy life on the open range before they are shipped to feedlots. People against grazing on public land should give it a second thought, as that time in the animal's life is their best time. Contrary to false beliefs, if not overgrazed, range cattle improve the carbon cycle by adding organic matter to the soil and stimulating vegetation's growth just like the vast herds of bison did before human impact. Having learned from the past, most ranchers do not and cannot afford to overgraze anymore. The standard rule is usually to leave half and then move on to the next area. Alan Savory, a brilliant scientist who has managed elephant herds in South Africa and studied the impact of herbivores on the environment for decades, says that the number one and most effective way to reverse carbon emissions in agriculture is natural grazing of herbivores. He came to the conclusion that the killing of 40,000 elephants a few decades ago "to reduce desertification by overgrazing" caused the opposite effect! Today, he claims that the most efficient way to bring carbon back into the soil is through regenerative and well-managed grasslands with ruminants, something nature did before humans interfered on a large scale. His twenty-minute Ted Talk is very explicative. So, please let's respect the management of free-range cattle on public lands, which is about the last way to produce food naturally and preserve our landscapes and the climate.

When it comes to industrially raised poultry and hogs, some simple facts should open our eyes. Just the odor which emanates when boiling and peeling low-priced industrial eggs tells us where they come from: closed buildings where the air is saturated with ammonia and H2S from manure. The tens or hundreds of thousands of animals or birds are crammed into the strictest minimum vital space possible without daylight and fresh air. The ventilation in these buildings is for survival but insufficient for quality meat. As everything is a matter of habit, industrial eggs' smell is most likely what most of us expect an egg to be. It is the same with chicken meat, which lost considerable amounts of nutrients and therefore also flavor over the past decades. Part of the tragedy is that after a generation or two, we don't know better and even prefer what we are used to eating.

Broilers, chickens "designed" for meat only, are strongly selected for breast muscle development, the most marketable part of the chicken. They are so deformed that they cannot move much and must lie around most of their final days, dragging their breasts and bellies in the manure-covered ground they are raised on and lose part of their feathers doing so, making them prone to infection. Many of those who fall on their backs can't get up anymore because of their deformity and die that way. Industrial chickens, broilers, or layers are fed GMO grains and need antibiotics regularly to survive.

Compare this with open-air free-range chickens, feeding on all kinds of bugs and seeds and supplemented with organically grown whole grains and without antibiotics, like Joel Salatin from Virginia, has demonstrated for years. Wouldn't it be a smart and wise choice to eat half as much chicken and spend the same amount of money on it? It is an alternative that adds significant quality of life on all levels; soil, carbon footprint, pollution, health, and quality of life for chickens and yourself.

Next time you order or buy chicken, think about it. We have to realize that knowing these things makes us obligated to act more responsibly.

Many people firmly believe that the stress and anxiety from industrially raised animals are transmitted to us and will consequently cause us ailments.

Suppose we do not change our consumption habit of industrial meats and do not change our attitude toward animal husbandry. In that case, more and worse diseases will occur. We are challenged and need to be more aware of our consumption! For health and environmental reasons, we Americans need to reduce our meat consumption by a minimum of 40 percent and consume instead quality animal products raised respectfully and naturally. The current high animal protein diet recommendation is a fad and will fade away. Is it a coincidence that we Americans have been greatly affected by COVID-19? We cannot blame others and point fingers at the "industry" because we are the industry if we consume these products. We are what we eat!

Plant-based and Synthetic Meat Alternatives

Plant-based and synthetic meat is a fast-developing market. Many who have good intentions to support the environment have praised it, including Bill Gates and the World Wildlife Foundation. As Bill Gates is the largest farm-land owner in the United States today, we can hope he will convert his holdings into organic production to underline his serious intentions. Organic ingredients would also make plant-based meat more attractive, of course. If done like this, it would undoubtedly be a significant improvement for the environment rather than current industrial meat production.

As mentioned before, food matter and its chemical composition is such a complex thing that even science cannot understand much about it. In this case, the wisest way is to follow the wisdom and intelligence of nature itself. That means observing nature, understanding nature, copying nature, and applying its rules.

If there is one single thing you take with you from this book throughout your life, it should be to trust nature's wisdom over our human brains.

As some people effectively do very well on a strict plant-based diet, obviously, plant-based meat can be sufficient for them.

As plant-based meat is also a processed product, it leaves the door open to many abuses, such as being produced with GMO grains and therefore with herbicide traces and the addition of processes and ingredients unknown to most of us. Organic plant-based meat would undoubtedly be more trustworthy. But why not simply eat plant-based proteins like whole beans, peas, soy, and oils? At least then we know what we eat. Remember: "As simple as possible, but not simpler," said Albert Einstein. Rice and beans cover the food base of a significant part of the world population very well. Still, it is insufficient for some, such as for people with physical outdoor activities during cold and dark winter months. It is a fact that plant-based meat does not furnish enough or very little of some necessary nutrients such as iron, zinc, B12, essential fatty acids, and creatine, which has been studied extensively for its ability to enhance athletic performance and play an important role in cognition (Avgerinos et al., 2018).

Life-cycle analyses also suggest that the novel plant-based meat alternatives have an environmental footprint that may be lower than beef finished in feedlots but higher than beef raised on well-managed pastures (Stephan van Vliet, Scott L. Kronberg, Frederick Provenza; USA, 2020).

Our personal choice at home is to consume meat from organic grass-fed herbivores and keep our meat consumption at a reasonable level, which means not eating meat every day. We have no problem with organic plant-based meat substitutes, but we certainly do not trust synthetic meats. How can any rational thinking person trust the "business" of lab meat? Without any doubt, our choice at home would be vegetarianism rather than consuming artificially processed and lab-grown meat. How could anyone buy this product after observing the constant increase in health and environmental issues caused by industrial agriculture and the food industry? The thought of laboratory produced meat shows how removed we are from nature and is a sign of the end stage of a civilization: Decadence.

Observing and understanding nature helps to overcome much of our intellect-induced confusion. How could sixty million bison in North America, besides the millions of elk, deer, moose, pronghorns, and other ruminants, have caused "human-induced" climate change before Europeans settled the continent? Bison, which are very similar to cows, were destroyed by immigrating Europeans within one century, reduced to 157 animals by the end of the nineteenth century! Today, there are approximately ninety million head of cattle instead and 360,000 head of bison. In the United States, the increase in large herbivores over the past two centuries is in ratio much less significant than the increase in methane world-wide during that same period. Where does the additional methane come from? If cattle are a major cause, it is largely due to the burning of Amazon forests to be replaced by cattle production.

Methane is, of course, also caused directly by fossil fuel burning, and indirectly by the manufacture and use of synthetic fertilizer. Nitrogen fertilizer causes the deterioration of organic matter in the soil, which releases CO_2.

The only action we can take is to change our human behavior and activity. That means to stop deforestation; to cut down immensely or eliminate totally fossil fuel burning; to reduce our meat consumption by almost half and to completely avoid any industrial meat consumption.

Cows served humanity greatly for millenniums. They have suffered a lot in our hands, especially today by enslaving them to milk machines and force-feeding them with junk food in containment. And now on top of all that abuse, we blame them for our problems? Shame on humanity and our "science"!

The most advanced scientists usually conclude that nature's way is much superior to our intellect.

Making a Change

If anything, it starts with us. It starts with each individual. That is where we need to improve, modify, and change. We are that tiny little trickle that contributes to the big rivers and lakes and, ultimately, the ocean. Trying to change someone else does not work. We have to be the first example. One day a lady asked

Mahatma Gandhi if he would advise her son to cut out sweets. Gandhi agreed but said that he would talk to her son in three weeks only. He was there at the appointed time, and the mother wondered why he waited for three weeks. Gandhi said that he could not tell her son to stop sweets until he had stopped eating them himself first.

Suggestions can be offensive. The German word for suggestion is *Vorschlag,* which translated means literally: pre-hit. We are all apprentices of life, and just like in school, we are all in different grades and learning different processes. There are first graders and university attendees. Does a college student criticize a child in elementary school for his limited knowledge? If anything, the college student will instead help if needed. We will find that same pattern in all areas of life, food production, and consumption. No adult is going to debate about nutrition with a child. Parents will feed their children as well as they can and will explain simple things. But vegetarians or vegans and hunters can have big debates. These can result in a paradox. Some are so passionate about not harming animals that they would just about kill hunters if they could get away with it (!?) On the other hand, abusive hunters are totally ignorant about what they are actually doing. Families with limited financial means surrounded by an abundance of game who harvest some of it for food know what they are doing and are usually responsible.

How hypocritical we can become in our debates about our personal point of view is well reflected in the endless and fruitless debates between Democrats and Republicans. Problems are generally, if not always, about human nature. Though different policies, systems, or techniques won't solve the root of the problem, they result from mutual and fruitful cooperation. They are necessary to apply our inspirations and ideas and, therefore, improve life.

So how can we individually contribute and help improve our food source? Whoever has sufficient compassion for others, animals, and the environment is most likely already living responsibly. Here are some ideas for easily applicable actions for those sitting on the fence and who question if and how they can practically contribute. There are undoubtedly many more or better ways, as some suggestions are also time sensitive. Most important is to *do* something. We need to make a genuine effort without being fanatics!

Air: the Most Eminent Need for Life

Remember that industrial fuel-based agriculture is the second highest producer of carbon in the air.

- Improve the carbon cycle by reducing the consumption of fossil fuel:

- As Americans, we need to considerably reduce our meat consumption and instead produce and consume quality animal products respecting the natural laws.

- Consume solar food (organic) as much as possible. Avoid industrial meats altogether and adapt your meat consumption to your real need and not what commercials or diet recommendations tell you. Don't eat meat every day and adjust it to your age, activity, climate, and season (less in summer, warmer temperatures, and older age).

- Don't waste food!

- Reduce airplane travel as much as possible and take road trips instead. Air traffic emissions have been identified as possibly one of the most significant contributors to climate change. Let's do our homework on this matter. We need to do business meetings via visual telecommunication such as Zoom, Skype, or others; to walk, bicycle, car-pool, or use public transportation to work.

- Adapt vehicles to our real needs with the best fuel consumption possible or, even better, an electric car. The best would be an E-car charged by solar or wind power. But even charged with fossil fuel or coal, the fossil fuel energy efficiency is considerably increased. Fuel engines put 15 percent of the energy on the wheels; electric cars charged with a source of fossil fuel put 30 to 32 percent of that fossil fuel energy onto the wheels. That means more than double the mileage!

- Heat our homes with solar or wind or use wood or wood pellets as fuel if locally and readily available. Burning wood does not throw the carbon cycle out of balance because it does not transfer underground carbon to the atmosphere like fossil fuel does. Those sources of carbon are meant to remain naturally underground and not brought to the surface and burned.

- Find an independent engineer or technician who will help you save money by reducing non-renewable energy consumption for your heating. You can accomplish this by better insulating your house, placing the heat source at the optimum spot, recycling lost heat, and using more efficient appliances.

Water: the Second Most Important Element for Living

- Reduce your consumption of bottled water as much as possible. Drink water from the faucet and use and refill the same bottle! If concerned about water quality, use a filter to eliminate undesired pollutants and chemicals and add a device to revitalize water. (Grander system, magnets, specific stones, etc.)

- Be aware of your water use, especially in arid areas and during droughts; reduce your consumption to strict necessity; minimally water the lawn or replace it with more drought-tolerant plants and trees. Wash the car with less water and less often or wash it on your lawn or close to a tree in need of water. (P.S. other people care much less about the looks of our car than we think). Sweep the driveway instead of rinsing it off; convert an unused swimming pool into a vegetable garden by filling it with soil. It can be converted back to a pool later.

Farmers:

1. Reduce your irrigation to the minimum possible: Study the methods.

2. If you can, farm organically or use synthetic fertilizers only to compensate for the specific nutrient lacking.

3. Don't "junk-feed" your crops with synthetic fertilizers; it makes them thirstier and more susceptible to frost and fungus diseases.

4. When changing your tractor's or combine's oil in the field, do not drain it into the soil; collect it, and recycle. (1 gallon of oil pollutes 1 million gallons of water!) Minimize or eliminate groundwater pollution with livestock concentrations. For example, bale-graze cattle in the winter instead of feeding at the same place all the time. If forced to keep feeding at one place, do it under a roof and bed the animals to avoid runoff into the groundwater. Use the bedding to fertilize your fields and compost it first, if possible.

5. Avoid concentration and spilling of synthetic fertilizers and pesticides.

6. Practice regenerative agriculture by keeping your soil covered.

Soil and Food

"Live with the land, not off the land!"

–John Middlemiss

When it comes to food, we have to remember that we wield a lot of environmental, economic, and even political power with our forks and spoons. The choice of consumption that is at our disposal provides us with much more power than we think! Most of us do not realize how much. Our economy could be improved and turned around to better and more sustainable ways within a few months by adopting some basic changes in our consumption. Most changes will not affect our comfort and will not inconvenience us but will improve our personal lives.

- Do something! Don't be extreme, but do enough, so you know that it would make a big difference if everybody would do that. Be an example.

- Use your intellect only to differentiate nature's way from the human commercial way. For example, to recognize whole and natural foods as opposed to processed foods.

- Use your senses, gut feelings, and inspired guidance to tell you what foods you and your family need. Recognize what is healthy at this moment for your family. Be consequent but not fanatical and make a distinctive difference.

- Use common sense to buy what is economically and environmentally appropriate.

- As much as possible, buy food without ingredient labels or with a maximum of five ingredients.

- "Eat food, not too much, mostly plants" (Michael Pollan)

- Buy organic and locally grown food and produce in season whenever possible.

- Go to the farmer's market.

- Cook at home as often as you can.

- "Cook like your (great) grandmothers did" (Michael Pollan)

- Grow your own food as much as possible. Growing lettuce and herbs in pots on your balcony is a good start and use organic potting soil or rent a space in a community garden near you. If there is enough space in your yard, have some chickens, and if enough land, also grow some fruit trees, maybe have a couple of goats or a cow for milk and dairy products.

- Grow your vegetable garden organically: Never apply synthetic fertilizers, but composted manure or other compost, bone meal, fish fertilizer, and mulch instead. Use natural botanical pesticides and fungicides like Neem oil and others.

• If you farm, also grow your own food as much as possible. If you farm conventionally, think about reducing chemicals considerably or even switch to regenerative or even organic methods.

• Buy meat, dairy, eggs, and farm fish from responsible producers. Avoid industrial animal products of any kind as much as possible, for the sake of the animals and the soil; the preservation of organic matter (carbon).

• Leave room for exceptions; when invited, honor your host or hostess and eat what is served you.

• Give your children good examples and the right education. Have at least one family meal per day together at the table; not on the couch, nor in front of the TV, or around electronic devices. Sit together at the dinner table.

• If you live alone, occasionally invite a friend, a family member, or a homeless person for a simple and healthy homemade meal.

- Make your main meal a daily celebration and something to enjoy.

- Pray or meditate before eating. Show gratitude after the meal by doing the dishes or leaving a good tip to the waitress if eating out. Most of all, let's show gratitude by improving our responsibility toward consumption.

Be aware that whatever we do and consume, we are deciding how to invest our time and money and then we justify it with facts.

Necessary Modifications and Improvement of Our Industrial Agriculture

- Education: Ag students should base their knowledge on real science, based on observation of nature and not on commercial science. Be aware that most public colleges are directly or indirectly subsidized by related and financially interested industries. Colleges and universities should not be commercially oriented, and organic farming methods should be taught in agricultural schools at the same level of excellence.

- Fair market prices instead of subsidies to grain farmers! This switch would have to be done carefully and step by step to allow farmers and the grain industry to adjust. Subsidies are one of the fundamental problems in large-scale farming. It is an absurdity, and socio-economic sin supported and financed by our government for the food industry. Their only purpose is to compete with more cost-effective producers internationally and control the world grain market. Huge grain farmers would make little to no profit in an average year if the government didn't subsidize them. Citizens are not aware that they pay taxes on cheap food indirectly in the form of subsidies. Some conventional and honest grain farmers literately admit that they "produce crap" and that they would be bankrupt in a heartbeat without subsidies (see the documentary "King Corn"). To add insult to injury, the larger part of grain production (GMO and herbicide immersed) is used for livestock and much for grain-fed cattle in feedlots: What an absurdity from Alpha to Omega!

• Organic farming should remain a free choice but needs an improved infrastructure that allows a more direct route from farm to supermarket, farmer markets, and consumers. Restrictions and regulations in general agriculture should be established to protect consumers and not to protect the ones controlling the industry. Most food regulations are for the protection of big corporations rather than to protect public health.

"The food industry does not care about public health, and the health industry does not care about food,"

- Wendell Berry

If it weren't so, GMO grains and crops covered with glyphosates would be illegal, and glyphosate would not have been approved as an antibiotic in 2010 (!?) Farmers need more protected rights for producing, marketing, buying, and using the seed they want. We actually need more restrictions on pesticides and fertilizers. One of the few and most essential restrictions should be the amount and type of fertilizers applied.

- Substantial reduction in nitrogen fertilizers. A limit of fifty pounds nitrogen units/acre/year (=110 lbs. /acre of 45 percent urea) should be imposed. Inducted ammonia in gas form is a major factor in burning organic matter and releasing carbon into the air. The above-indicated amount is more than sufficient to maintain the proper carbon/nitrogen (C/N) ratio and provides more than enough to cover any lack or surplus for the plant's need in relatively healthy soil. Synthetic fertilizer should only be applied when there is a deficiency and as a supplement, not as a default plant food. Organic farming confirms that the number one thing the soil and plants need for proper growth is a good soil aggregation/structure for good water infiltration and an active nutrient cycle with a high population of mycorrhizal fungi. Synthetic fertilizers and pesticides are counterproductive to these soil characteristics. Independently thinking scientists and engineers, who are not paid or sponsored by the agriculture industry, say that soil will never become sustainable as long as the standard high rates of synthetic fertilizers are applied.

Once nitrogen (N) fertilizers are limited, the need for other fertilizers like Phosphorus (P) and Potassium (K) is also reduced. The lack (or rather its imbalance and blockage) of micronutrients such as zinc and iron, for example, becomes practically nonexistent. It is the balance of nutrients in the soil which is essential. Too much nitrogen in the soil is comparable to an imbalanced human diet with fast absorbable nutrients like refined sugars or fats. The strong dominance of synthetic fertilizers, especially nitrogen, causes a relative insufficiency of other nutrients and, consequently, weakness and vulnerability to illness and pests. Experiments I did as a technician in agriculture showed me that balanced or organic fertilizing of nitrogen makes crops more resistant to frost, drought, fungus, and falling!

- Banning some pesticides used in large-scale agriculture such as SDHI fungicides or bee-killing insecticides such as neonicotinoids. Several pesticides are much less harmful and have proven no resistance to plants and insects over time. Examples are copper for downy mildew, sulfur for powdery mildew and rust, neem oil as a general pesticide for fungi and insects, pyrethrum and powdered rotenone as an insecticide (harmless to warm-blooded living beings).

- Banning GMOs. Not everyone knows the long-term negative impact of GMOs on health and the environment. Many GMO crops are strictly modified to be glyphosate (RoundUp) and/or 2,4 D herbicide resistant. It is not a sustainable approach because the crops are sprayed regularly with these very questionable chemicals. The plants may be resistant, but people are not, as we are finding out more and more. Are we currently in the process of sterilizing our soils? It might be sooner than expected that some soils will simply not produce anymore or only with dramatic and high-cost input. The GMOs relationship to herbicide resistance is most likely an unnecessary intervention with no real economic advantages for the public, and a disaster for the environment in the long run. If the same amount of time and money had been invested in mechanical weed control, use of cover crops or optimized crop rotations, our soils and therefore human health would certainly be in a better state.

• Combined farming with crops and livestock should be supported and promoted. Animal dung is and remains the best fertilizer for plants.

• The majority of farms and ranches should go back to reasonable family-operation sizes, where the combination of livestock and crops can be handled by the members of the family and occasional help.

• Manure lagoons should be limited in size and be 100 percent leak proof by law. Ideally, these lagoons should be underground. The size of the lagoon and the quality of the manure should be such that the farmer can spread it over his fields without concern for the environment.

Manure and money have something in common. If spread out on a large scale, it nourishes all, but if piled up, it will starve and pollute its surroundings!

Don't Be a Fanatic!

It is very disgraceful when someone turns down a meal the host has prepared with a lot of care and attention for a special occasion because of rigidity in their diet or philosophy about food. Allergies have to be respected, of course, as well as vegetarians.

Americans have a reputation in the world of being extreme or puritanical in whatever they do. It may be a strong point at times, but it is often a drawback because life is not black or white; it is mostly in the gray zone. The great majority of people are somewhere between being abstinent or being an alcoholic. Most of us are not either-or because there are countless levels in between. Like with anything else, what is bad for us is the habit. When I first came to America, I was often surprised to experience that people either did not drink alcohol at all or would drink too much. I am still surprised to see social events and dinners without beer or wine. The aspect of liability interferes, of course, but it is a strange approach to make others responsible for our own faulty behavior. One notices this unusual approach when not raised in America. In most countries, it would never come to mind that the host is responsible for their guest's alcohol consumption. The concept that assault-weapons are available in stores for youths at age eighteen or that a person of that age can go to war but cannot buy some beer is beyond any understanding outside US borders. I was forty-five years old when a cashier asked me for my ID as I purchased a bottle of wine! (?). There are a lot of very well-functioning, responsible, and very productive people who drink regularly. Driving tests have shown that a person who consumes alcohol regularly may act and react way more "soberly" with double the amount of alcohol in their system than a young person who is not used to the effects of alcohol.

I am a firm believer that anything we do every day and without exception is not beneficial to us and is an addiction. The bad thing about drinking, smoking, or snacking is the habit. All that can be part of our lives and serve us well, as long as it does not control us.

Feel Your Nutritional Need

Feel your needs, don't think them! As omnivores, we can eat just about everything. Toxicity or benefit is most of the time a matter of amount. Too much raw organic broccoli can intoxicate us, and cyanide in the smallest quantities like in almonds or apple seeds is beneficial to our health. Some highly processed food and beverages sold in our supermarkets definitely require more restrictions and discipline in consumption if we want to remain healthy. Sadly, that is how it is with much of the food offered on the market nowadays. To put it simply, safe foods in the supermarkets are without an ingredient label: produce, grains, nuts, fish, meats, basic dairy products, oils, vinegar, spices, etc.

The more something is processed, the less we should eat of it. As we all should know by now, processed foods are high in sugar, refined carbohydrates, and trans fats. Fried foods, pizzas, pastries, highly processed cereals, candy bars, ice cream, etc., are not toxic in the short term but should be a small part of our diet. Again, it is not about all or nothing but all about quantity, frequency, and alternation. Let's not be fooled by what that means and realize that health requires daily discipline. Home cooking or not, essential natural foods should be the bulk of our diet. The rest should be considered treats. A commodity pizza can be a treat for convenience when there is a lack of time, but it is not nourishment. Instead, a piece of good organic bread and cheese with a V8 vegetable juice is just as convenient, certainly healthier, and not more expensive. And despite all that, yes, it is still enjoyable and fun to go to Pizza Hut occasionally. An occasional (whisky) coke can do wonders and hit the spot perfectly after a hard day's work. But if pizza and a coke become a habit, they lose their effect and can't be appreciated anymore and will cause harm.

We have been inundated by commercials for industrially processed foods. We have been so misguided by false information that we fell into the temptation of more convenience and consequently lost the link to real nutrition connected to our landscapes. Anyone who has ever had a perfectly ripe peach on a hot summer day after strenuous physical activity when water does not quench the thirst anymore responded to the body's natural request, which asked for electrolytes and essential nutrients peaches specifically provide in that situation. When eating a ripe and juicy peach in season, which is the hottest time of the year, we do not need to know about electrolytes! They are in there, and our body intelligence and taste buds know that the peaches are full of it.

This body intelligence must be based and developed on *natural (!)* foods, starting in the earliest stages of life, ideally during pregnancy. The later we have to recalibrate our body intelligence, the more difficult it gets. This fact translates again to simple home cooking. Conventional ready to go meals and processed foods are also filled with artificial flavors and colors, fooling and misguiding our taste buds and our basic instinct to satisfy our real nutritional needs. Someone who has eaten industrial chicken all their life will most likely and unfortunately not appreciate pasture-raised and nutritious broilers. It is very unfortunate when somebody grows up eating mostly processed foods, that this person may never really regain the ability to know their real need spontaneously.

Be Aware of Your Food Sources

There is a good chance you missed out on the experience of enjoying a fully nutritious fruit at its peak of ripeness. That is not your fault, as fruits in the supermarket are usually not local anymore and are picked unripe to survive long shipping distances. If the fruits are grown with synthetic fertilizers, which all of them are unless specified organic, they will have little flavor or are even unpleasant to eat. Also, modern varieties are selected for longer shelf life, which usually means tougher fruit, something no living being prefers besides the people marketing it.

Big and weak food makes us look the same way in the long run. Good tasting fruits can be found in the supermarkets toward the end of their season, and better if organic. For example, strawberries from California usually taste much better in May than in March, which is the beginning of their season. In general, farmer's markets are a better source for finding quality produce. Organic dairy, eggs, and meats can be of top quality at supermarkets as shelf life allows a little more flexibility. Today, many farmers will ship their sustainably grown and frozen meats directly to consumers. Fish should preferably be wild-caught or farmed organically rather than genetically modified and fed with GMO grains and antibiotics like "cheap" salmon are.

Respecting the Gift of Our Body

It is an act of love to respect our body, which has been given to us. It is an act of love to oneself and others, for the simple fact that we are all connected and that our actions and consumption impact others. Yes, we need to consider our bodies as a gift, though we have full responsibility for them. The body is a working tool given to us temporarily to manifest our desires and accomplish our apprenticeship in this earthly life. What have we done to "earn" our bodies? Nothing really, or nothing we are aware of, besides satisfying our physical needs to breathe, eat, keep our body within a suitable temperature range and multiply ourselves by satisfying our sexual drive. As our body is a gift, it is our duty to respect it. The rewards are health and joy of life when respecting our body without overdoing it and falling into obsession. On the contrary, our lives can turn to hell or even suicide if we don't. As adults, we can express our gratitude for a healthy body by accepting the responsibility of new life born to us and passing on what was given to us.

Food for the Mind

Who am I?
Caught between the past and the future
Between endless space outward and inward
Temporarily limited with the great gift of a body
My only field of action being the Here and Now
With the only option to say Yes or No to whatever
presents itself
Stunned at times about my nothingness in all of this
But realizing my belonging to the All and to the Always
I can only be part of a Creator
Just like you, my brothers and sisters!

This poem came spontaneously to my "mind" the night of my past birthday; as if somebody had spoken it out loud to me. I got up and wrote it down.

Curiosity, Interest, and Challenge

The appetites of our mind are curiosity and interest. Our mind, just like our body, needs to be adequately fed to grow and function healthily. What feeds our mind? It certainly seems like feeding our minds becomes more of a challenge for our society nowadays, as is feeding our bodies. Unbelievable and instant access to everything on the internet is overwhelming and confusing. Just like our bodies, our minds can also be "overweight" and intoxicated. Carrying extra and unnecessary weight in our minds causes stress and often leads to depression, as our minds beg for rest and at the same time, our souls beg for attention. Constant screen time, background noise, social media, and relentless advertisements are major offenders.

An undernourished mind will affect the fulfillment of our life's purpose and result in a lack of satisfaction. A healthy mind will go hungry if not fed.

So, what is good food for our minds? The mind's appetite is generally expressed by interest and curiosity. Too much curiosity becomes the mind's gluttony. Interest is related to the spirit. Spirit is the source and origin of our mental state and our expression of physical life and actions. Life, in general, requires us to activate our bodies and tame our minds. The Peaceful Warrior keeps telling us to tame our minds.

Any form of education is undoubtedly the main ingredient necessary to feed our minds and is, of course, acquired mostly by life experience through all physical, intellectual, and spiritual activities. Education requires self-discipline and proper action.

Discipline is an indispensable trait to help nourish the mind properly. It requires effort and needs practice and is not always enjoyable. No matter the outcome, it still bears fruit one way or another. The Quaker, Richard J. Foster, defines in his book Celebration of Discipline the twelve steps of discipline for spiritual growth in a wonderful and practical way. Several sources have qualified this book as one of the ten best books ever written. If you have limited time to read, I recommend putting aside the book you are currently reading and switch to Foster's Celebration of Discipline!

Overindulging the mind is very tempting with all the available technology and easy to do with Facebook, Twitter, etc. The Internet can be a fantastic contribution to our lives and is neither good nor bad in itself but neutral. It all depends on what we do with it. If used with discipline and responsibility, it is probably one of the greatest assets around. It adds additional comfort and challenge at the same time. Poor discipline on the internet can become self-consuming and can take on a life of its own, slowing our real progress and satisfaction in life. We all have to find out where the limit is between information, confusion, and addiction. More is not better, and life is mostly about actually doing something. Unnecessary screen time very quickly becomes counterproductive!

Keeping a connection with friends and family, having a sense of humor, and sharing opinions are vital. But too much social contact quickly becomes hectic and wears us down more than we think. Do all the jokes shared on the screen really keep us upbeat for very long, and does all the sharing of opinions help us move on in our lives? Does online reading about positive thinking make us think positively for the rest of our lives?

The Peaceful Warrior explained in a "Ted Talk" two different and fundamental approaches to the search for a balanced and harmonious life: "First you need to quiet your mind, so you can create empowering beliefs to raise your self-esteem so you can practice positive self-talk to find your focus and affirm your power to free your emotions and visualize positive outcomes, so you can find the courage to generate the confidence to make the determination to form the commitment to feel sufficiently motivated to do whatever it is you need to do" . . . and he ends with a big sigh "Whew!" . . . and said that he instead recommends the second approach, which goes like this: "Just do it!"

Philostro said that there is much more to do than to know.

The Work on Oneself

To work on self is an essential part of life. There are different ways to do it. Good mentors and leaders in life show us that it is not complicated. They offer and recommend keeping it simple, which does not mean easy. But it is extremely easy and tempting to get lost in that journey by spending too much time reflecting on oneself, thereby running the risk of missing the train of opportunities. It is comfortable to get trapped in spending much time on self-search with the excuse that we are accomplishing meaningful work. Self-search can become addictive. Discussions with alcoholics under the influence is predictable and boring for the people around who prefer to do things rather than talk about them. An efficient tool to get over being stuck with self-absorption is to lift our heads, look outward, and see what is in front of us and what needs to be done first. Afterward, we can do what is possible, and soon we will do the impossible. Once we work for others as much or more than we do for ourselves, we know that we "belong," that we are more united than we imagined, and we realize that life becomes lighter and more joyful. That change of mind might be difficult at first hand, similarly to the most challenging moment to go for a run is the time it takes to get off the couch and out the door. The rest usually happens by itself, and satisfaction is one of the rewards. In contrast, making plans to create a fantastic project to help humanity and change the world is so overwhelming that the outcome is usually no action and will most likely end up with more navel-gazing.

Start Small!

It is much more efficient and useful to run around the block instead of just planning a daily ten-mile run. For anything new, start small, quietly, and gently! As we pick up the routine, the amount and the speed will increase very naturally. To avoid being self-absorbed, we need to begin to think about others slowly. We can easily do little and kind things like dishes, raking an older neighbor's leaves, a short visit to lonely or sick folks. Simply paying attention and listening to the person who talks to us and to value their point of view without imposing ours is a significant contribution to helping others.

As the action of "doing" is of vital importance to the self, it might seem a paradox to say that life is much more about relationships than about achievements and is less about what we do but more about who we are.

Relationships and Sexuality

Most adults desire a great partner with a good sexual relationship. As this is what we hope for, we also need to provide the same to our partner.

Suppose we have the illusion that our partner should or will compensate for our shortcomings. In that case, a relationship is not going to happen or survive long term.

The purpose of marriage is neither to be happy nor to be unhappy. If we are not content with our single life, we won't be satisfied in a relationship. It is an illusion and irresponsible to expect consciously or unconsciously a partner to solve our problems. Marriage is for mutual advancement. Our spouse is usually our best mentor. Let's also not forget that our improvement in life is often the result of resistance and opposition.

Falling in love is a helpful fire starter. It is the kindling that ignites the logs. As we all know, this period is usually short-lived, which does not mean that a relationship is meant to become dull. Logs can burn pretty hot if they are replenished and fed with plenty of fresh air! So, let's keep feeding that fire and leave plenty of air and space to our partner.

Spiritually and in accordance with the nature of gender, a man is supposed to love (to provide for) his wife as much as he is able, and his wife is supposed to respect her husband. If one of the spouses does not fulfill this expectation, the other cannot do it either. This starts a vicious cycle wherein she can't respect him because he does not love (provide for) her, or he cannot love (provide for) her because she doesn't respect him. Couples often remain stuck there due to a lack of genuine and honest conversation. Lack of communication is the central problem in a couple. Also, we have to realize that love is not gazing at each other, but it is about looking together in the same direction. A common spiritual outlook is an essential foundation.

How does someone "find" their soul mate? The day we realize that we will not find the perfect soul mate, but that we have to mutually grow together is also the time we are ready for a relationship. Still, as a single person, the choice of partners may seem limitless, and that is why we need to limit ourselves. Do we really "choose" a life partner, or does it just appear like that? As so much in life seems to be orchestrated from behind the scenes and because there are no coincidences, how much choice do we actually have? We certainly have the freedom to say yes or no to any relationship. Still, long-term partners usually know that they were put together. Though, as in anything else, we have to help ourselves so that Heaven can help us. To find a partner, we need to have an open mind, be ready for the responsibility, and ask for guidance.

General good advice for a young man who considers a serious relationship or marriage is to observe and learn from the future in-law's family background and watch the dynamic and emotional formatting. Family patterns very often repeat themselves over generations. Good and harmful behaviors are passed on. There is a good chance that your future wife will behave and act in a similar way as her mother. If the mother of the lady you envision as your future wife is faithful and respectful toward her husband and loving toward her family, that is how your future wife most likely will be. If there is no mother-in-law around because she left her family for another man, there's a chance that you will probably raise your children by yourself later on.

For young ladies, watch how your partner or future husband treats his mother. Watch how he talks to her and how patient he is with her. That is most likely what you are going to get. Whatsoever, we all have work ahead of us when we incarnate in the family of our choice. It is part of our evolutionary work we consciously accepted at some point. We have to grow and advance in our capacity to love. As we all have freedom of choice, it is the refusal to do so that will repeat the same unfortunate family patterns and make them even worse. Some people need more time to choose the journey of love than others.

This world is a school, and marriage is one as well. Suppose we refuse to consider that and prefer to live without responsibility, without any effort to improve, and egoistically take advantage of everything and everyone. In that case, we will inevitably hit a wall. Often, it is the necessary shock that helps us to evolve.

The problem is that our current society wants docile consumers who are made stupid with consumer slogans, not people who look at life with their hearts.

Sex is a potent energy. Like any other powerful energy source, it must be handled with much care and discipline. Sexual energy has substantial leverage both ways. A lot of good can be created with it, obviously and ultimately new life. But it can also cause much harm, destruction, and death. So young people, let your horses run free and fully in the open and designated fields but hold onto them in town.

The desire to find a partner is healthy, natural, and necessary. Philostro says that there is not one good reason for single life and that we have to give back the life we have received. He values the life of a couple who love each other to the end as a great masterpiece.

The Benefit of Talking and Undertaking Less

Have you ever noticed how at times, after a long conversation, you feel like there was no substance to it, that it had not inspired any participant and that it instead made everyone feel uncomfortable, empty, and worn out? Ever notice how sometimes after a very "busy" day, you had the impression that not much was done and that it was an unproductive and unfulfilling day? There is a good chance you talked too much or undertook too many unnecessary projects or both. Did you ever notice that when it happens over a prolonged period everything becomes tasteless, just like food does when we continuously eat and snack?

The consequences of continuously overloading the day with unnecessary additions cause stressful feelings of emptiness and lead to depression. It might even be a trigger for cancer in the long run. To drown our feelings at the bar on nights or weekends may help us forget occasionally, but we will not get relief over time.

Life is an exciting journey where there are no coincidences or accidents. If we do what life presents to us and requires of us and simply answer by yes or no, we have done enough for the day. And the present day is all that counts. Very interestingly, we will experience more fulfillment and life intensity that way. We often worry that we might miss out on something or on good times, and consequently, our actions are driven by stress and anxiety and become counterproductive on the level of satisfaction. Of course, there is also space, need, and comfort in light and easy conversations around the table. Still, like everything, the limit lies in the boundaries of our consciousness. Once we realize that, we have more responsibility to act within those boundaries, by talking less to say more and undertaking less to do more. The corona virus lockdown was a great invitation to realize and apply this, and by doing so, we "turn shit into fertilizer." At the peak of the pandemic, news commentators questioned when things would be going back to "normal." What is normal? Back to packed airports with endless waiting lines at 5 a.m.? Back to be stuck in traffic for hours, daily? To be buzzing around all day doing what? To keep looking away when we are driving by lines of tents filled with homeless people in our big cities? Going back to an excess of "bread and games" and making the rich richer and the poor poorer? We all consciously or unconsciously know that our society is going at high speed toward self-destruction with our current lifestyle. Like my brother once said, "We are driving our vehicles at one hundred miles per hour toward an upcoming wall, and we still have conversations about the functioning of the wipers."

Quality Versus Quantity
of Communication

It is highly valuable and stimulates our minds to communicate with like-minded people and mentors regularly. If we can't find them around us, telecommunications allow us to find the people we need quickly. We have to be sure to regulate that! Over the past two years, I have had the most interesting and stimulating conversations with a scientist, author, and professor in agriculture I had met only once before. Our discussions are by email only and on a regular basis. But here again, if our telecommunication is of superficial value and without restriction and discipline, we become enslaved rather than enlightened and liberated. Listening to motivational speakers, mentors, and good music can be very stimulating. We really need to protect ourselves from distracting and polluting our minds with too much news, commercials, sports events, TV shows, or constant background music. Our minds need rest just like our bodies, not just sleep. Our current society has a great tendency to underestimate that! We may be "doing" much more than we think by occasionally just sitting on a bench in the park, on a log in the woods, or the balcony of our apartment doing absolutely nothing for a couple of hours. Walks alone in the woods or city parks provide great and "active" rest for our minds. Be kind to yourself and give your mind a daily break when possible.

Art

Art is probably as important as breathing. We can't neglect it. It is a very stimulating activity that binds the mind and soul. I recall how good it felt to be in a choir when I lived in hectic Los Angeles. It was such pleasant food for the mind and peace for the soul. It is also very relaxing to watch and listen to Bob Ross's painting and life lessons on TV, but it is more proactive to grab a paintbrush!

Music is a form of language and food for the soul. Just like there are very different ways of communicating and types of food, there are very different kinds of music. There is not only wholesome music but also junk and intoxicating music. Like anything else, we have to be aware of what we consume, and responsible for what we produce. Music can be healing and inspiring to the point of enlightenment, as it can also be destructive and addictive. As fun, happiness, and joy touch different parts of our whole being, so does music.

Classical music like Beethoven, Mozart, Vivaldi, Handel, or Bach has passed a long test of time. It touches many of us deeply, heals greatly, and can bring profound joy. Many people, especially young people, do not care for this type of music or even dislike it. Good classical music reveals the state of our soul, anywhere from joy to depression. Lighter music like Country, South American vibes, Jazz, or Polka touches us differently and can make us very happy. Rock and Pop touch us more physically, a good example being "Elvis the Pelvis." Just like alcohol, powerful Rock music should be consumed in moderation. Rap music, a dominant form of popular music today, is all about repetitive lyrics. Even when one is not consciously listening to them, they are having an impact. Violent, sexually exploitive, socially destructive, and hateful words, even if only registered subliminally, will do damage. Creative and inspiring lyrics will benefit humanity, and sometimes throughout history. Songwriters are often poets who use their single musical instrument to provide more expression to their life messages.

Be conscious of intoxicating music. GIs in Iraq were shooting from their tanks at women and children listening to Rammstein, a band named after the 1988 Ramstein-airshow disaster, a mid-air collision between three stunt planes that killed eighty people. They added an "m" to the band's name, which gives it the meaning of "ramming rock." We need to be aware of what we consume! Heavy metal, trashy rock, and similar music are addictive! Consuming this daily is destructive.

Art is such a vast field; from all kinds of music, painting, or poetry to activities like cooking, landscaping, redesigning the interior of our home, or rebuilding muscle cars. To follow what attracts us spontaneously and naturally is where our talent lies. As we know, there is the temptation for art to fall into the trap of money or over-intellectualization. Whatever we do, let's not turn our art into a chore, but rather our chores into an art.

Mind-altering Substances

"Work is the curse of the drinking classes."

–Oscar Wilde

Unfortunately, recreational drugs, prescription drugs, alcohol, nicotine, and caffeine are substances many of us regularly consume to attain a more pleasurable state in body and mind. Suppose we are healthy and not in chronic or significant pain. In that case, it is a very slippery and dangerous slope to elevate our sense of well-being with drugs to get "high." The effect is very temporary, and the after-effect brings us lower than we were at the starting point. Doing so is beyond a lack of wisdom. As everything is a matter of amount and frequency, any of the above can also be beneficial. But let's not be fooled and use this as an excuse for excesses. We are naturally programmed to function best without any of it.

Alcohol has been around and has been part of many cultures forever. It is the simplest and most common form of a mind-altering substance. Without human intervention, any mass of any fruit or moist grain will naturally convert its sugar into alcohol, fruits into wine, and moist grains into beer. It is vital to notice that any of these naturally fermented substances have on average ten times less alcohol than manmade and more sophisticated distilled wines (brandy), distilled beers (whisky), or distilled bulbs (vodka). Alcohol in its natural state was already prevalent in ancient Egypt, especially in the form of beer. Beer was made from barley with honey, herbs, and spices and was drunk in preference to water. After all this time, certain cultures developed a genetic tolerance or even a specific need for moderate alcohol amounts. In moderation, it stimulates the spirit as it raises blood pressure and reduces some pain temporarily. There are plenty of old sayings about alcoholic beverages dating back from ancient cultures like "Water for the skin, milk for the bones and wine for the blood," or "He was a wise man who invented beer." – Plato, or "Beer is proof that God loves us." – Ben Franklin.

"In Vino Veritas" translates to "In wine is the truth." It means that people become more authentic with alcohol consumption and show their true self in body language, behavior, and words.

During my career selling wine, I experienced on a daily basis how people's true soul state reveals itself when consuming alcohol. Talkers start to talk, funny people become funnier, happy people begin to sing, angry ones start to fight, and sad people begin to cry.

Folks with centuries or millennia-old traditions of fermenting grapes, grains, or tubers will always accompany any significant event with an alcoholic beverage. In business and deal-making, it is often used subconsciously to check the person's honesty or veracity. Also, the Bible has its comments: "Wine rejoices the heart of men and jewels the heart of women," and "wine was poured to loosen the tongues." Alcohol accompanies most parties and celebrations to increase the good mood and ease communications. Wine and beer in moderation are also stimulants that encourage hardworking laborers at times. Napoleon said: "No wine, no soldier."

Where Is the Limit?

So, where is the tipping point between beneficial and detrimental? We all have to find out what works best and helps us thrive, but self-control is inevitable. Discipline is the little window of resistance or effort required that shows up once in a while, which we have to endure for a relatively short time to benefit significantly in the long run. If there is no self-control while consuming alcohol, accidents, illness, or failing relationships are not "accidents" and are major warnings. Many souls try a journey of alcoholism, sometimes over several lifetimes (if we believe in reincarnation) until they have suffered enough. Then they realize that they are on a dangerous dead-end road and will have to change or stay until an accident or a major drama occurs to put an end to it.

In oenology (winemaking) school in Switzerland, they told us that we have a problem if we cannot be four consecutive days without alcohol. One of my clients was director of the drug and alcohol department at the CHUV hospital and medical research center in Lausanne, Switzerland. He said that it is essential to refrain at least one day, preferably two days per week from alcohol. A healthy limit for an average adult is the equivalent of two to three deciliters of wine (eight ounces) or two regular size beers. Cultures with a long history of alcohol consumption say, in general, that none should be consumed at all until past puberty. Later on, a self-learning process is necessary, of course, and there is hardly anyone who did not experience at least once a lack of control and a bad hangover. Philostro says that a simple medical cure for alcoholism is to drink vinegar. I assume that this might work best if wine is the primary alcoholic beverage consumed by the individual, as wine was just about the only form of alcohol in France at that time.

Wine and beer are a wonderful gift to humanity if consumed moderately and such a tragedy when abused.

Tradition

It is not only wise to listen to our inner voice but also important to pay attention to our physical and emotional responses to our consumption of stimulants. Education and the support of social and local traditional culture are usually a road map for healthy guidelines. When young people are exposed to proper driving, proper handling of dangerous tools or firearms at a young age, they will have a better chance to handle these things responsibly later on. It is the same with alcohol. Obviously, and for many vital reasons, we cannot serve alcohol to children. Still, we can pass on education at a relatively young age, mostly by our good example. Cultures with old traditions of beer or wine will start to familiarize their children sometime between the age of reason (seven) and puberty with their traditional beverage, but more in a symbolic way. For example, in the old wine-producing countries of Europe, parents will pour a little sip of red wine into their child's water glass. The amount of alcohol becomes totally irrelevant, but there are two strong messages in doing that. First, it gives the children the encouraging message that they are starting to be grownups. Second, it helps develop a sense of responsibility by showing and saying each time "Only a little," and this on repeated and regular occasions for the children to get the message.

As parents, we need to teach responsibility very early and be an example first. The following scenario may surprise Americans: Switzerland is a country with an old tradition of obligatory military service. It is a young soldiers' obligation to keep their assault weapon at home and keep it after they complete their service. Please note that at the same time, a Swiss can only purchase a gun in a specialized store with a spotless criminal record. When I was a kid, we participated in the youth sports shooting program at fourteen years old. We went with our bicycles and a military assault weapon provided by the army on our back to the shooting stand. I never heard of any accidents, which was, of course, the primary reason this program existed. As a young soldier, I also recall that on Sunday evenings, as we were heading back to the barracks, the train stations were full of soldiers with guns everywhere. Again, I never heard of any crimes or accidents. That works only if there is an experienced tradition without any abuse. Unfortunately, that is not the case in America. Hopefully, that will change.

American Puritanism

Americans retain a somewhat puritanical culture, which has its pros and cons. Whatever the cause is, our approach is often "all or nothing," good or bad, black or white. Whisky was dirt cheap and freely available until Prohibition. It might be slightly exaggerated, but we tend to think that someone is either an alcoholic or a teetotaler. Let's be aware that there are many degrees of alcoholism. What determines a problem is the habit of drinking and therefore losing freedom by dependency. No one is "pure," and everyone has hang-ups somewhere. It could be more coffee than needed, a sweet tooth, or overeating in general. That is just human nature. Common sense and listening to our quiet inner voice, listening to our surrounding family, and real friends will keep us from unpleasant consequences.

We must also accept that accidents are not accidents but incidents to help us change and improve.

Recreational Drugs

Consumption of recreational drugs is a relatively new and widespread phenomenon in our Western culture. What a sad chapter in our days! In the United States, tens of thousands die by overdosing on opiates every year. So many young people fall into that trap. Certainly, young people need to discover life. Still, today's easy access to a big choice of drugs and their cocktails on the black market as well as pharmaceuticals like Oxycodone, Hydrocodone, and especially Fentanyl is devastating. In America, the consequence of misuse and abuse of pharmaceuticals is by far on the top of the list of premature deaths. Several years of experience working with youth programs, where most of the inmates have a history of recreational drug use and medicated drug abuse, brought me to the following simple conclusion: It is the result of hungry and thirsty souls! Whenever a new boy arrived at the program and who was "using," I always asked them: Why did you get into drugs? The first answer is always "I don't know." Digging a little deeper and asking why they did not resist the offer the answer is always "peer pressure." When asked if they did not realize that they were harming themselves, if they were aware the damage could have lifelong and irreversible consequences for the body and brain, the answer is always "I honestly did not care." Aren't these answers the writing on the wall?

These boys are willing to step selfishly and fearlessly over health and family relationships for something they believe is better. What they are really trying to do is to avoid emptiness, loneliness, and boredom. It is a partial suicide. They also are looking for acceptance, in other words looking for love. When hanging around users and partying too much, many teens give in easily to temptation and step on the slippery and deadly slope. Sadly, and much too often, they never fully return.

I used to describe the youth program where I worked part-time as "a home for troubled teenage boys," but now I instead call it "a place for boys from troubled homes." Professionals all agree that the root of the problem lies on all three levels; the parents, society, and the youth.

How Can We Help?

Raising and dealing with adolescents has never been easy for parents, but it seems more of a challenge in the current times. It is a masterpiece when couples love each other and stay together to the end and raise their children with affection and discipline. Besides holding to clear limits, insisting on house rules, and accepting this approach's consequences and rewards, the best education is to be a permanent and good example. The joy and pride of couples who put much effort into their children's education can be seen on their faces and clearly shows at events and family gatherings.

Some parents have the unfortunate misconception that they should supply all the needs of their children. That is a big illusion and helps no one! As we all know, it is more helpful to teach someone how to fish than continually supplying their need for fish. Indeed, parents have to nurture, protect, and provide necessities and affection to their children. But tough love also plays its part at times. With some exceptions, children should have to earn everything which is beyond their basic needs. It is a recent and unhealthy tendency for some dads to want to be buddies with their sons instead of being the authority figure. As parents, we know that it comes very naturally and that it is easier to spoil the children rather than restricting or training them. Of course, this also requires more work and time from the parents.

Unfortunately, nowadays, most couples have to work full time to make ends meet and sadly some control their children with medications. Lack of time and focus from the parents causes behavioral issues. I recall what the owner and manager of a youth program, who has been successfully operating for over twenty years, kept saying to the boys: "You are here because your parents never told you No!" If parents don't actively participate in the living dynamic of a disciplined give and take, set clear limits, and most importantly, be good examples, families dry out and fall apart. Parents staying together and pulling in the same direction is the foundation for children's successful upbringing. We will approach this issue in the next chapter.

Naturally, children are bored easily and are looking for something fun to do. Overdoing screen time and electronic games is ultimately not fulfilling. Play, entertainment, and parties are necessary parts of life but do not provide durable satisfaction and become quickly detrimental when overdone, which happens sooner than later. Consuming recreational drugs will never compensate for the lack of life intensity and can be a route of no return! It will make things worse very quickly. The price of short "highs" is enormous, even more than anticipated by our society and of course, youth believes itself to be invincible. As a young teenager, our school took us, class by class, to an exhibition done by a neighboring high school. The hall showed many big black-and-white posters of overdosed adolescents and young adults lying dead or unconscious in public restrooms or on the side of the street. These addicts, especially the men, looked skinny, weak, and dirty. Very sadly, it showed the reality of lost and wasted youth. The impact of that school project affected many of us. Surprisingly it did not work for others.

Of course, young people have to go through life experiences to grow and learn to evaluate what is good and right for themselves and ultimately for others. The problem with drugs is that the individual's undertaken journey is at high risk of no return, leading only to misery or death. The only way out is to call for help.

Life is love and is always present when we are ready to accept it.

Food for The Soul

Our birth is but a sleep and a forgetting;
The Soul that rises with us, our life's Star,
Hath had elsewhere its setting
And cometh from afar;
Not in entire forgetfulness,
And not in utter nakedness,
But trailing clouds of glory do we come
From God, who is our home

—William Wordsworth

To be kind to one another and to accept true love is the most difficult learning process in this world. It is the biggest challenge in life, but the most rewarding as well! That is why we are here and why we should do kind things even to our enemies.

This chapter will inevitably touch on mythological and spiritual approaches. Despite the common denominator of all religions, which is based on mutual love, charity, and brotherhood, we are all strongly impregnated by the specific religious values of our upbringing. Our American Constitution was constructed on Christian values. Christian values represent every religious denomination in the country that is following the teachings of Christ. The Ten Commandments are written in stone and visible to the public in our Nation's Capital. Fervent atheists and rebellious and anti-religious individuals or movements unconsciously and willingly follow Christian rules and regulations and gladly submit to our laws based on these values. If people commonly say that something is "right" or "good," it is usually based on their country's religious values.

Therefore, many of the approaches presented in this book are influenced by this cultural point of view. If America had been predominantly Buddhist, the book would have had more of a Buddhist approach, as simple as that. Without imposing our convictions, we simply use the tools provided and familiar to us. Everything has a reason to be, and God leaves us free choice in our beliefs.

Christians, their leaders, and followers have committed many grave wrongdoings throughout history, and Americans have participated in our fair share of abuse. Using the Bible with selfish and cynical motives was recently on display during the George Floyd antiracist demonstrations. Of course, this behavior has to be rejected, but the baby should not be thrown out with the bathwater. No healthy mind can disagree with the central universal teachings of Christ at the Sermon on the Mount.

What Is the Soul?

Christianity states that spirit and soul are two different entities. Philostro says that we cannot really understand what the soul is. To make it more easily understood, he sets the soul somewhere between the spirit and the (emotional) heart. To grasp the difference between soul and spirit is not easy and remains a mystery to most of us. In ancient Hinduism, Atman means "eternal self" and is often referred to as "spirit" or "soul," therefore no obvious distinction. In Buddhism, Anatman or Anatta means "none-self" or "no self." The soul, as it perceived in the Christian culture, is hardly ever mentioned or almost ignored in Buddhism. These facts show how difficult it is for humans to understand what the soul is and what the difference between soul and spirit really is.

If comparing our being with a computer or a smart phone, the device would obviously represent the body. The spirit seems to be the operator and the necessary electricity might be comparable to our physical energy and our soul.

In a similar way, the Swiss author and school psychologist Dr. Beat Imhof compares the body with a car, the spirit with the driver, and the soul with the fuel.

The fact that we can feel physically, mentally, and emotionally is another indicator of the existence of the trinity of our being; body, soul, and spirit.

The native Chinese, Watchman Nee, who first introduced Christianity to his country, says the following in his book The Christian Life and Warfare—"In conclusion, the soul is the source of the personality. The spirit is the part with which man communicates with the spiritual realm. The body is the part with which man communicates with the physical realm. The soul is in the middle of these two parts. It exercises its judgment to determine if the spiritual realm is to rule or if the physical realm is to rule. Hence, the soul has to authorize the spirit to rule before the latter can rule over the soul and the body. The reason for this is that the soul is the origin of the personality. Hence, we can say that the soul is the personality."

The Choices of the Soul

In the previous chapter, we saw how our society, in general, has deviated from natural and healthy foods. Why has our society evolved this way, and what made that happen? That is a very fundamental question. There are many different answers, depending on who we ask. Some people will say that the current food situation is the best humanity has ever had. It may be true in the short run for some of us. There has never been such a tremendous quantity and choice of foods in industrial countries as there is today.

There are as many opinions as people about the situation in our current food industry. Whatever the reason for the decline in food quality is, most people who see a problem will spontaneously say that greed is the origin of the cause. Conclusively, this is as close as it can be to the root of the problem because people are not dumb. We know better.

Greed is selfish because it is about "more for me and less for you." It is the engine for excessive personal profit in money and power. Industrial and commodity-oriented agriculture profits only a few while the primary workforce at the base of production is treated as part of the commodity. The quality of the outcome speaks for itself.

The word for greed in Christian mythology is called avarice and is considered one of the seven "deadly sins" next to pride, anger, gluttony, sloth, lust, and envy. Our current culture has an aversion to the words "deadly sin" because they negatively connote the institutional Church's power and abuse of authority by inflicting fear and guilt. Today, a more popular term is "to make poor choices." However, it's called; these seven temptations are traps and something we all have to deal with in this world.

The spirit is timeless. It never rests. As our soul gets "older," we realize with time that these temptations are dead ends and which we are allowed to experience in our multitude of lives. Over time, we slowly start to give up on poor choices based on the repeated negative consequences of these experiences.

Indifference is the state of a lack of life experience and the state of a young soul. It is the polar opposite of mutual kindness. In other words, indifference is the opposite of unconditional Love. Love is driven by compassion and understanding based on life experiences. Love is life, life is movement, movement is action, and action is about doing things in this world. The opposite of life is inaction. Philostro says that it is better to do bad than to do nothing. He also says that God loves bad people. The scriptures say: "So, because you are lukewarm, and neither hot nor cold, I will spit you out of my mouth." Committing bad (poor choices!) or wrong actions is something we stop doing after a while because the consequences we harvest just become too painful in the long run. With pain, we become compassionate and progressively reverse our actions to goodness and kindness to ourselves and others. Over many lifetimes our actions slowly and gradually move toward what is Good, Right, and Beautiful for *All*.

Choices and Their Consequences

In the industrialized Western world and especially in the United States, we have been taught over generations to make a profit. The emphasis on profit has become almost our primary religion. America first; profit for the company and self, first. Worse, greed has been praised and identified as something good to strive for by individual economists and politicians. No wonder we are having problems. Greta Thunberg's speech to world leaders in September 2019 included: "We are at the beginning of mass extinction, and all you can talk about is money and fairy tales of endless economic growth. How dare you!" She exposes our race for profit and our fear of inconvenience very explicitly. What does it mean when the President said that we have to "Make America Great Again?" Does this underline that we are not "great" anymore? Would this kind of understanding of change really make us "great again?" And should that "greatness" be just for us? If so, this could end up being nothing else than selfishness in a globalized world and might lead us to ruin in the long run.

Interestingly, Philostro said in the late 1800s that America would isolate itself from the rest of the world and suffer the Egyptian plagues sometime in the future. What that exactly means is not clear and cannot necessarily be taken literally as described in the Bible. Still, it is surprising how America has been distancing itself from the rest of the world and how climate disasters have drastically increased in force and frequency over just the past few months or years. It is not impossible that we might also suffer an invasion of locusts decimating the whole Midwest's crops as climate changes and bugs are becoming resistant to insecticides. As Bill Gates mentioned in a TED Talk in 2015, diseases and the threat of virulent viruses will most likely be the next form of the plague.

America was probably at its civic peak from the nineteen fifties to the eighties. It was most likely a result of our country's truly great actions done previously: sacrificing 400,000 men, hard fighting, and hard work to save Europe from a totalitarian regime. The war was followed by the Marshal plan, a financial aid program and other initiatives, sponsored by the United States, designed to boost Western European countries' economies after the Second World War. That is what made America great! That is what made America a super nation. No surprise that twenty years later, we were the first to put a man on the moon. Indeed, supporting our allies also had some self-interest behind it, but overall, what was accomplished far surpassed any self-interest.

Edgar Casey, who lived in Virginia Beach around the beginning of the twentieth century and is known as an illuminated medium, said that our nation's sin is to have set high ideals and standards but not followed through on them. Our forefathers' well-meant guidelines and indications can also be twisted and turned around to harm, as scriptures have often been used to justify wrongdoings and even atrocities. Didn't our government invade Iraq with a Bible in hand and, after much destruction, come back, exclaiming "mission accomplished?" But the reality was different. The second Iraq war is seen by many as an invasion of self-interest, costing several hundred thousand deaths that remain on our collective conscience. Many peaceful Muslims will admit that their extremists are also misusing their holy scriptures, the Koran, to justify atrocities.

Consciousness of Our Actions

I recall a successful Chinese businessman from California telling me that he was asked to give his company a motivational talk. In his presentation, he said that his key to success was and wrote the word in big letters on the blackboard, LOVE. Of course, there were a lot of cynical smiles and comments in the audience, he said.

A significant reason for that reaction is simply because the word "Love" has been partially distorted over time.

In contrast, the fact that business leaders tell us to think through finances to understand the world shows the emphasis on personal profit in our society. Having worked for many years in the financial world as a commodity futures broker, I see money as a neutral form of energy that has to be handled with respect. We can use it to build orphanages or concentration camps, hospitals, or weapons for our allies and our enemies. There is a black market for recreational, addictive, and very destructive drugs, and there is the business of essential and necessary medication.

Fear Trumps Rationality

We can harm ourselves and others consciously or unconsciously. What causes us to harm others always comes from a selfish motive. It can be indifference, greed etc., but is also often the result of fear. Fear can eradicate our senses, creating extreme irrationality. Based on polls, many people are more afraid of public speaking than of death itself. The fear of loss of "power" and "freedom" is often expressed by emphasis on the "right to bear arms" in America. This fear very sadly leads to the loss of many children's lives in our schools. Fear can certainly be justified and can be a vital servant at times, but it is because of a lack of faith that it can enslave us. It is a lack of trust in the process and faith in divine guidance. I find it interesting to observe that the kind of fear that arms itself with guns is more prevalent in the country's rural parts where Christian religions actually dominate, an apparent paradox. Isn't fear the only thing we should be afraid of, as one of our greatest presidents said? If you want to be encouraged and inspired by a man with courage and faith without limits, I highly recommend watching the documentary Mully. This Kenyan man's life and journey help us understand the statement that if our faith would be the size of a mustard seed, we could move mountains.

We Are What We Eat

There is a correlation between the food we eat, the activities we engage in and the personality we have. "Tell me what you eat, and I will tell you who you are" or "You are what you eat" are familiar statements and say more than it appears. A logger requires different fuel than a scientist or an artist. Very often, authors or creative minds are vegetarians. There is a good reason for this. Some people (still) know instinctively what kind of food they need. In my observation, it seems that a vegetarian or vegan diet "sharpens the tool." It sharpens the mind and allows a more sober connection to the spirit, and increases sensitivity and creativity, despite the spirit's direction. A logger or construction worker does not need these faculties as much, but a composer, an author, a scientist, or a strategist does. Renowned artists have confirmed that they need a vegetarian diet or one low in animal products to be more inspired and creative. But "sharpening the tool" does not make us a better person. Improved creativity and sharpness can be used to either create or to destroy. Remember that Hitler was a vegetarian, and that the Dalai Lama eats meat.

Our personality and state of soul will determine and choose what kind of food and the amount we will ingest. Gluttony or eating disorders are usually indicators of an unsatisfied soul. The same manifests itself on the positive side through the ability to enjoy meals and also to celebrate with a feast at times, while simultaneously having the ability to fast periodically. The type of food we chose to eat and our consumption, in general, indicates strongly what our soul is hungry for and by what kind of spirit it is inspired. Indeed, and as mentioned, our activity impacts our diet considerably, but people with the same activities and lifestyles may also eat quite differently. Our type of appetite is not a coincidence or just the result of genetics or biochemical reactions and their combinations in our bodies. It is the other way around: Our body is an expression of our soul and spirit. I recall one of my farm bosses saying that people work as they eat. I observed that efficient workers also eat efficiently, hardly snack, sit down for dinner at the same time each day, and leave the table as soon as they are done. They want to get things done. That does not mean that they cannot enjoy a dinner party or that eating faster is better, but if somebody is lingering over their plate for a long time, that is how they are most likely going to be at work as well. Vice versa, certain types of food, besides the use of drugs and stimulants, have a specific impact on our personality. Philostro says that we should restrain from eating the brain and heart of animals because they have "too much of the animal in it," as he simply explained.

When questioned about eating pork, Jesus said that it is not what goes in our mouth that defiles us, but what comes out of us, like our offensive speech or lies. In other words, our primary concern should be about our thoughts, words, and actions rather than food. Harmful and destructive thoughts, harsh and offensive words, and immoral and violent deeds will not only hurt others but do indeed intoxicate our whole being and make us sick in the long run.

Images of Chinese saints and sages of the old times and the Chinese representation of Buddha, one of the great spirits of this world, are shown as somewhat over-weight in our modern concept. It apparently does not necessarily hinder spiritual greatness. In contrast, it is written that John the Baptist lived only on honey and locusts. Franciscan monks during the Middle Ages fasted every year before Christmas and Easter for many days and every Friday of the year! St. Francis suppos-edly did a fast of forty days. Antoine, a close friend of mine, does a complete fast of thirty to forty days every year. He has done it for about thirty years and, at the age of sixty-five, has above average and perfect physi-cal and mental health and is still working full time in a hospital. People with the experience of fasting over a more extended time recommend that one should know exactly what they are doing and why they are doing it. After about three weeks, the fast apparently reaches a different dimension, and meditating and praying be-comes an indispensable tool of survival.

All these approaches conclude that there is a corre-lation between our physical and spiritual appetites. A mystical and philosophical approach says that it is "the soul which feeds off the earth." As absurd as it scientif-ically sounds, it seems to make sense somehow in that perspective. If not, where do eating disorders originate? Or why do not more people follow a good and healthy diet, as most of us pretty much know what that consists of? What we are hungry for physically reflects what we are hungry for in life and reflects the state of our soul. Certainly, there are many unknowns, but the fact that science remains on a purely material level inevitably creates a conflict with spiritual and mystical points of view. Hopefully, some of these reflections will inspire some hungry souls to step onto a different path leading to a good spring of water and real nourishment. Most importantly, let's remember that the experience is worth tenfold the knowledge, and as Bruce Lee said, "Knowing is not enough, we must apply. Willing is not enough; we must do."

The Spirit of Our Food and Health Industry

Many people trust our food and health industry a little too much and do not want to be bothered by inconvenient questions. Sadly, this means willfully giving up our power and self-control concerning our health. Often, we hear, "They say this is good for you. . ." Who are "They"? How far do we go before we do a little research or give some thoughts and healthy judgments of our own to some of these statements? If we cannot be bothered, later as health problems arise, we expect the doctor to find the right pill for a hopefully quick cure.

Daily we get brainwashed and bombarded on TV with "ask your doctor."

It is very gratifying, but it takes a little discipline and effort to do our homework and control or improve our dietary habits rather than giving our power to "the doctor" or profit-oriented-corporate science. Spiritually, to give away our self-control is a result of sloth, while "giving up" is a lack of faith. The likely consequences are, one medication may follow the next because of side effects, and of course, the person becomes a financially lucrative patient for the medical business. The root of the problem remains undiscovered, the problem is not solved, but from a purely financial point of view, we become "good accounts" rather than patients. We will never have a sound health insurance system for all, as long as medicine and health insurance aim for corporate and personal profit and as long as the system is abusive on all levels. It is simply impossible! Curing the sick should not be profit-oriented but a service to others. Despite this and looking on the positive side, surgery today is at a very advanced level. People pulled out of car wrecks with numerous fractures, sometimes even temporarily clinically dead, etc., are being put back together and onto their feet to fully functioning persons within weeks or months. Antibiotics have saved so many lives from bacterial diseases.

During the COVID-19 pandemic, we saw very hard-working and compassionate nurses and doctors. They show the most heroic physical and spiritual behavior. Some insurance companies probably try their best to survive the harsh competition, while others profit tremendously at the same time.

We have gotten trapped by our system. It is not possible to pin-point the responsible individuals because it is a system-wide failure. Of course, some are certainly more responsible than others. Solutions and changes for all citizens to have adequate access to health care have to be applied within the whole system and in the entire nation. That means we need more consciousness and awareness. It is the same for our food industry. A vastly improved_education for all is a fundamental key for that. Unfortunately, it is not in the interest of a corporate-run government that folks are well educated. The fact that we currently rank seventeenth worldwide in general education after high school while being the world's wealthiest country confirms that. We used to be first decades ago, at the time when America was flourishing.

Most likely, any health care system would work just fine if everyone would not abuse it. It has a lot to do with a general mindset and the abuse and lack of responsibility on all levels. At the bottom, patients have to make a genuine effort not to abuse the provided services and medications. Doctors should not push for medication, treatments, or medical tests to cover liability issues and for personal profit. A part of that behavior is a result of unconsciously being caught in the system and trusting it. Education, especially in the medical field, is supported and sponsored by big Pharma and based on profit-oriented science. I recall Elisabeth Kuebler-Ross, an internationally renowned doctor who once said in the nineties: "Today our medical students have educated themselves to imbeciles." As already said, we have many fantastic and responsible doctors and nurses and accountable and disciplined citizens, but not enough of them; otherwise, we would not be the victims of our system. It is easy and convenient to follow the direction of the profitable industrial complex. Unfortunately, and at the same time, not many realize that we are enslaved by technology to a significant extent; it is controlling us instead of us being in control of it. I can hear Elisabeth Kuebler-Ross saying again, already in the early nineties, that nurses spend more time behind the computer than with their patients.

What is the cure? It is the courage to change ourselves first, the courage to think more independently, act more responsibly and be more responsible toward others and the system. It is also about embracing the discipline of sufficient education. Persistence and patience are the keys. We can do all of this without being fanatics. "Keep our feet on the ground and our head in the skies," as the Peaceful Warrior says.

Different Souls, Different Personalities

We are all different and behave differently, but we are all meant to be healthy. We are all relatively similar in looks, but we can be light years apart in our behavior. Desires and actions can vary immensely from one person to the other. At first glance and from a distance, some of the mass-shooters may look very similar to wonderful people. Some top athletes don't look that much different than some couch potatoes, when in a suit or a lovely dress.

So, what makes that big difference? If it were only a matter of our brain and intelligence, there wouldn't be simple people who do extraordinary things or highly intelligent people doing hugely destructive things. Where do our desires come from, and what drives people in one direction or another?

Philostro said that our thoughts come from the heart and that the brain only reflects on how to put ideas into action.

As mentioned above, our desires can vary immensely in motivation:

We may have a neutral desire to go for a walk or a cynical desire to rob someone, or a positive desire to help a neighbor or to adopt a healthier lifestyle. The brain's job is to put these desires into motion, but the brain itself has no desires, nor does it create anything. Good or bad ideas are delivered to our individual or collective spirits. Our soul, say approves or disapproves the idea and then the brain reflects on how to put the action into motion. Finally, the body executes it. This procedure is not taught or discussed much in traditional medicine because science is relatively limited in its knowledge by remaining on a purely material level and also often motivated by self-interest. A little over a century ago, Philostro said that humans are at the first letters of the alphabet in terms of scientific knowledge. It seems like we have progressed with a few additional letters since then, but we certainly are still far from reading, not to mention understanding. Dr. Alexander Eben is an American brain surgeon who had an unbelievable personal OBE (Out of Body Experience) and was himself brain dead for two weeks. Besides his incredible journey, he also concluded how limited the understanding of traditional medicine is when it comes to essential questions about life and death. With his message, he helps open minds and explores new territories full of hope and joy. He illustrates it very well in his book Proof of Heaven.

Taming Our Minds and Pushing Our Bodies

As the brain will reflect upon putting needs and desires into action, there may come a brief time of satisfaction with our achievements. When satisfied and not pushed by vital necessity, humans tend to put reflection and progressive actions on autopilot and focus more on consumption and enjoyment. "Bread and games" then seem sufficient for many. Life is often a struggle because that is how it is designed. Whether we accept this fact or not, or however we want to call it, if we drop our guard for too long, we will experience the consequences sooner or later. As a result, we can lose our family, job and personal freedom. On a larger scale, when we are too complacent, we risk being overtaken by another country through their dominating economy, by war or by a contagious virus.

Life on this earth seems to be a constant battle to keep our bodies up and our impulsive minds down. In other words, we need to stay active and tame our minds by holding our horses, being disciplined, gain awareness, and remain in control at the same time.

Any physical work or sport is ultimately nothing else than fighting gravity and working to keep our bodies strong. Taming our minds is spiritual work. Young men have a hard time respecting speed limit; money makers don't know when to stop speculating, and gamblers don't know when to stop playing.

The great disposition and discipline for taming our minds is patience. The American medium Edgar Casey kept repeating: Patience, patience, patience! This message was meant especially for Americans. The French mystic author Paul Sédir said: "One should be as patient as Hindus and as ambitious as Americans." Patience is not about waiting inactively, but much rather about continuous effort with faith to keep the desire in focus also when there is no wind in our sails. Faith is to trust the process and to know that we get the help we need. Trusting the process may take extraordinary courage at times. Philostro once said, "If you want to follow me, you will have to cross wooden bridges with rotten boards."

Connecting with the Spiritual Realm

Ultimately and in conclusion, our journey here on earth requires a connection outside of the material world. . . and it is not a Smartphone. This book does not intend to provide specific spiritual guidance or try to convince anyone of a particular belief system or religion. The intention is to realize that there is much more around us, much more than what meets the eye. Like so many others, this book is an invitation to stimulate personal and critical thinking, develop awareness, learn to evaluate ourselves, and find our own path on this journey of life. It is everyone's journey to search for truth. Life is least about the "haves and the have-nots," but rather about "to be or not to be," as was famously said.

I once heard a young businessman say to his grandfather that he did not need religion or God and that he was doing perfectly fine the way he was. The grandfather just said: "That is only because life is very easy for you right now." As explained previously, this young man, having achieved his comfort level, put aside his reflection about life. In contrast, my French grandfather, who was not a very religious man and never talked about God, went to Church most Sundays. Maybe meeting his buddies at the bistro afterward was an important factor and was another form of communion as well. As an eighteen-year-old, he fought in the First World War. He said that sometimes they had four to five attacks per day jumping into the German trenches, often with their bayonets on their guns; that they sometimes had to run over their own injured buddies and that often half of the soldiers fell in a single attack. One day, he and a group of twenty troopers were sent out to explore an enemy site nearby. Only two came back, one of them being my grandpa. He survived the war with bullets in his backpack and his gas mask but never got hurt. He once said to me that before any major attack, the field priest came and gave a blessing. He said he knew his buddies well and said that everybody, believers and non-believers, went on their knees for a blessing. Don't we also know from the Civil War that there are no atheists in the fox holes?

As an interesting side note, my grandfather always stayed a very gentle, balanced, hard-working, and even noble man with no signs of post-traumatic-stress-syndrome. Many of his surviving buddies did not show any significant post-war syndromes either. Asking my grandfather why that was, he said that they knew what they were fighting for their land and their own country. They did not have to live with the constant pressure on their conscience of unjustified killing. They did not participate in an unjust war or in an invasion of a country on the other side of the world like we did in Vietnam or the second Iraq war. In both World Wars, American soldiers knew why they were fighting overseas and were able to take a certain responsibility for it, before, during, and after the war. Yes, many had a hard time adjusting to regular life again, and some never really did, but deep down, they did not have the same pressure on their conscience. The high number of suicides of Vietnam Veterans speaks for itself. The responsibility lies strongly on our leaders, especially when the draft was enforced. On top of that, the survivors coming back were blamed by the Peace Movement! What a tragedy that was for America, but many learned a valuable lesson from it.

The End of Times?

The majority of people in the world, no matter their religion, believe that our times are due for drastic changes. Christians speak of the apocalypse and the return of Christ. The scriptures say that no one knows the hour or the day and that He will come unexpectedly, like a thief in the night. Other religions speak of the human cycle. Native Americans, as well as others, predict days of total darkness. The Mayan calendar going back several thousand years representing cycles of more extended human periods shows no more cycles after 2012. Based on several calculations and conclusions, world scientists set the Doomsday Clock to 100 seconds before midnight in January 2021. The original clock setting in 1947 was set at seven minutes before midnight.

As we can only change ourselves, why not be more aware and more prepared with body, mind, and soul? Curiously, it looks like the Super Bowl or the stock market is more of a concern for many of us. Despite that there is a feeling in the air that time becomes more urgent. And still, like the Wall Street markets, there is a tendency toward wishful thinking that the rising markets and the economy will continue like this forever. Part of this is because nobody knows when and how the market will collapse. Nobody knows when drastic changes will occur. So, shouldn't a specific preparedness and awareness be a constant certainty, especially nowadays? Wasn't it said that we have to remain alert at all times?

Corona Virus: A Challenge!

COVID-19 continues to impact the whole world. We do not know where it is going and when it will end. At the peak of the crisis, public events were canceled all over the industrialized world; schools were closed, air traffic was almost at a total standstill, the stock markets collapsed: indices fell 30 percent within a week and crude oil down to a quarter of the previous price. COVID-19 is a curse for the material world, and we don't realize that it is also an opportunity for the growth of humanity. Sadly, from a worldly perspective, casualties, and pain play a huge part, but it is necessary for growth.

Who ever thought that it could happen so quickly? It is a major challenge, but why should that be a blessing in the sense of an opportunity for growth? Simply said, it is an invitation for humanity to become more human. It is an invitation to share and do more kind service for one another and discover our humanness again. We don't live from bread alone. It is an invitation to stay "home" and stay "inside" and travel to our hearts, rather than travel everywhere worldwide. And it is already working. Republicans and Democrats were forced to work together more and were doing it. Great leaders and quality people we did not know existed will rise to the occasion. Doctors and nurses do heroic work and put their lives at risk.

People help each other and are more compassionate. Chinese cities were reminded of what clean air can be. These are some of the blessings, and this challenge represents the daily bread for our souls. It might look like more than we can chew, but it won't be. It may cost many lives, but humanity will grow out of it and become a little better and a little more compassionate, at least for a while. Yesterday the news commentator said that these kinds of challenges bring out the best in

Americans; in other words, a real opportunity to "Make America Great Again."

Beliefs and Opinions

Members of different churches who go door to door and try to convert people to their beliefs generally mean well. They often have good intentions. Even if we don't share the same perspective, it does not hurt to occasionally listen to them, just out of kindness and to honor their effort. And by the way, who says that our point of view is the right one? Does opening the door make us anxious about wasting time or getting sucked into something we don't want?

Good intentions are important and a good start, but not enough. We all know the saying, "the road to hell is paved with good intentions." Based on what some of these church members say, it is stunning to hear how easy it is to earn Heaven once and for all. For some, all one needs to be "saved" is to give lip service to the fact that they believe in Jesus Christ as their only Savior, to get baptized, and attend church weekly. Would a trained parrot be saved?

Interestingly, we can sometimes hear them say that we cannot earn Heaven with good deeds, but by grace alone. Didn't Christ say that we will pay our debt to the last iota and that every hair on our head is counted? Is it really that easy to earn Heaven as some evangelicals say and then "sit forever at the Banquet of the Lord" while others burn in Hell forever? Where is the love in this? Does selfishness belong in an enlightened state, or are there indeed seven levels of Heaven as mentioned in various religions and some Christian denominations? It is probably a blessing that missionaries and zealots who pretend to know the truth have not had more success. Philostro said a century ago that if priests and pastors would have no self or financial interests, that they would have whole flocks following them. Isn't it written in the scriptures that there will be big surprises and "grinding of teeth" on the other side? Of course, we like to think it is going to happen to the "other" ones. Philostro said once: "Heaven will not ask us what we believed but will ask us what we have done." Doesn't that make perfect sense and align with the teachings of good and enlightened leaders? Though, in what may seem to be a paradox, Philostro also said this about his uncle: "If he had believed, he would have been perfect."

For those who believe that there is a Heavenly Father, and that we are His children, let us consider the following: Do parents care more about their children's beliefs about who the parents are, or are it more important that their children obey them and are kind to one another? Would parents throw their adolescents out of the house forever based on what their children think of them, or would they rather temporarily put them in a youth program or another situation when they become too much trouble to keep at home? And by the way, all good parents will let them come back home with open arms once they turn around and behave again!

I participated in a conversation with a group of people years ago where the following question was raised: "When standing at the gates of Heaven and asked by God why He should let you in, what would be your response?" There were many interesting answers. But one response stood out and surprised some of us, as it came from a man who was not a churchgoer but who proved to have great faith in life and common sense with his answer. He said: "Because You created me."

Philostro once said, "All religions have to be respected and that ultimately in the future, all religions will melt into one of charity." He also said that charity does not consist of giving away all we have, but instead of "loving our neighbor as ourselves." In other words, love or kind service to one another will be the common denominator, not our beliefs. Philostro also said that Hell is right here on earth, which somehow concludes that Hell and Heaven are not locations but rather the soul state we inhabit. He also said not to be in a hurry to get to Heaven because "there is no one there yet and no one goes until we all go." Doesn't that sound very fair and encouraging and tell us that we are all in this together?

Isn't kind service to one another, more tolerance, and unity-in-diversity the key to peace and a brighter future? There are movements in the world going in that direction, for example, the Focolare, whose message is "Uno," which means "one" or unity. This movement follows the teachings of Christ but has open doors for every religion, where Jews, Muslims, and Hindus can be seen together with them. This movement surfaced in Italy after the Second World War, coming out of a time of enormous pain and suffering.

Unity is only successful if it is based on what is good, right, and beautiful for all; in other words, an upward direction benefiting and uniting the right and the left of this world. Uniting right and left without an uplifting direction leads nowhere and is not possible.

Mahatma Gandhi is an excellent example of a leader who fought peacefully for true unity. It is said that he remained a devout Hindu throughout his life. However, he was strongly influenced by ideas from several other religions and eventually developed many of his own unique ideas about religion, philosophy, and the right way to live. There is no contradiction in him being a devout Hindu who followed the teachings of Christ. Gandhi was a free spirit and an early adherent of the "one religion of charity" with kind service to all, without having to join any church. He was lucid enough not to throw the baby out with the bathwater, as he said: "There is nothing wrong with Christ, but it is the Christians I don't like." Like many great and courageous spiritual leaders, he had to pay with his life for it.

The following powerful message was provided anonymously online a few years ago:

(Translated from French)

My Religion Is…..

My writing is for the sole purpose of giving witness to the Truth
and trying to share as humbly as possible, without trying to impose anything, my own experience of God.
Understand well that no one can pretend to hold THE Truth and believe that one can introduce it to others.
So, do not cling blindly to my words, but rather seek to discover this Truth by yourself by searching at the bottom of your heart.
Take the time to push further to the knowledge of all things, turn to God, and surrender to Him and to Him alone.
For only His grace will make your inner treasure fruitful.
Ask and you shall receive, seek and you will find. (Matthew 7-7)
I have wandered for years in the world without knowing where to go, without knowing to whom I shall turn.

Lost on the market of spirituality, after four years of silence, here is the witness of my conversion.

Following a dream, upsetting in reality and revelations, my life has been totally questioned. One night, darkened with despair, overwhelmed by the insignificant weight of my life, frightened by my inability to become better, drained from the world and the wickedness of men, I addressed myself in one last attempt to God, asking Him to show me the way to follow, to continue to believe and to continue to live.

I then opened my heart and told Him of my misunderstanding.

Faced with these many contradictions that I noticed in all the houses of God, faced with all these constraints and all these ceremonies in which I did not want to participate anymore, ceremonies which, however sincere and useful they may be for others, could no longer nourish my spirit.

I actually ended up not feeling any more soul or love in all these gestures that I found executed too mechanically.

The feeling of hypocrisy before an invisible God isolated me more deeply in my loneliness and my disarray.

If you exist, I told Him. . . answer me!

Which way should I follow? Which religion should I turn to?

Do you want me to be Jewish, Muslim, or Hindu?

Where You are, I am going!

If You really exist. . . tell me! Do not let me die as an orphan!

Without response from you I would understand that you do not exist.

And then I just have to sink into facility, the meanness and the hatred and respond with evil to evil and to look for myself for a new god. . . or to finish with life.

Quite simply, I was more than determined and sure of myself.

At this very moment, a sudden fatigue took over and I dozed off.

This is where the extraordinary happened. A thing I did not believe in anymore, something that I did not think was possible.

Jesus, who is none other than the love of God, spoke to me, to me, the terrible.

Of course, such as a friend with a love imperceptible on this earth, a love such, that you are forever shaken.

His words were not like "Go there. . . or there, do such ritual, say that thing, be of such religion. . . or such other"

But He simply said: "Be good and be Love"

The next moment, barely awake from my sleep I began to transcribe with astonishing ease of writing all these words. Pushed by a supernatural force, and there, as I wrote, I understood with a deep and indescribable certainty.

I became aware of what my path should be, my belief and my journey.

All my intentions and all my will do not have any other reasons to be than to believe with all my heart, with all my strength, with all my soul and with all my mind in God our Father, our Creator and in Jesus Christ who is God Himself and who came to earth to save us and to liberate us.

Now, I make a point of trying to apply, somehow with each breath that is allowed me to have, with God's help and in front of all His works, through each of my thoughts, from my words and my actions the teachings of Christ.

Because now I know that the keys of the Kingdom of God are in me.

Here is the text that was inspired by our Lord Jesus Christ and as I wrote it to my awakening:

"My religion is Universal

Where there is Love, that's where my religion is

Where there is Peace, that's where my religion is

Where there is Mercy, that's where my religion is

Where there is Charity, that's where my religion is

Where there is compassion, that's where my religion is

Where there is respect and love toward all my Creation, that's where my religion is.

Where all my Creation works for Love, Peace, and Order, that's where my religion is.

Where your heart is crying for your neighbor, that's where my religion is. Where my messengers are preaching Love and Peace, have passed by or are passing by, that's where my religion is. Where we are without wanting to be, that's where my religion is.

My religion is like the water that runs through the smallest faults and brings life and resources. It is universal and accessible to all.

It is there, with each breath that you are allowed to have and ready for each of your words, of your actions, of your steps, of your crying, of your laughs, of your actions. It is just in you. I make my kingdom live through you. Give Him thanks.

You will know my kingdom through all that lives for love, through all that gives love, forgives out of love, helps with love, cries for love, and talks about love.

I will give you everything, all that you really need, only by love. Do not reject me.

Give me life as a mother gives birth to her child. Let me shine and breathe in you.

Set me free and you will be set free. Understand who you really are. You are made of love. And love just like water cannot become fire, cannot cause trouble, cannot become evil and cause suffering. This does not come from me, can't you see? See what I created, observe nature. It is the mirror of my kingdom. It is my Truth. Each creation applies its mission.

Nature purifies you, nature feeds you, treats you, guides you, makes you euphoric. Nature perfumes you, beautifies you, teaches you, guides you, warms you up, refreshes you, waters you, and loves you. And that is unconditionally.

I tell you in Truth, nature itself is crucified every day for your salvation, and this until the last of you recognizes its very own essence. Pray for them, because they suffer for you and by you.

I only ask you one thing. Be like a child who is hiding in the arms of his father, of his mother, to grow in love and trust. Take refuge in me. I who gave you Life, I will feed you, I will dress you, I will speak to you, I will teach you, I will protect you and I will bring you up to my side in order for us to be indivisible, by our nature and our image."

"Behold, the kingdom of God is in your midst" —Luke 17.21
"This Good News of the Kingdom will be proclaimed throughout the world,
As a witness in the face of all nations" —Matthew 24.14

The Power of the Institutional Churches

There are several reasons why many in industrial countries have walked away from church or mythology in recent decades. It is human nature that people distance themselves from spirituality when earthly life becomes more comfortable. Also, the abuse of power wielded by some clergy is not acceptable anymore, and rightly so. Sexual abuse of minors is evil incarnate and a monstrous disgrace. It is also understandable that many walk away from a religion that says a person who dies "unsaved" or committed wrongdoings without repentance in this single earthly life will burn in Hell for eternity. Fortunately, this doesn't fly anymore today. We have to be aware that humans will always harvest the consequences of their actions in this life and their lives to come, but the abuse of power through wrong teachings has no future.

Some avid bible scholars will say that it literally states in the Scriptures that "unsaved" souls will burn in Hell forever. That is the scribe's understanding and literal interpretation, as the Bible is called "the living word" and leaves the door open to different interpretations. Religious books are continuously misused to justify personal misconduct, wrongdoings, and to hold power over others.

Scaring people about Hell worked for a long time but fortunately, not anymore.

The new generations' hungry souls reject a cruel god and look for the God of Love, who can be found in all religions and all denominations. God does not change, we do, and our journey forces us to do so in a loving way.

We have to be aware that, at the same time, there is the risk of losing a healthy fear of God while rejecting misguided teachings. "Fear of God" is not meant to be a state of panic or distress. Christ said that He came to bring us Peace. A healthy fear of God is the vital understanding that anything besides faith and obedience to Love, to Life, and God is going against Life and ultimately against our best interest.

We cannot be humble enough and must realize that our short-lived, minuscule brains on this planet earth, wandering in an endless and timeless universe, do not have any possible capacity to grasp the complexity of Existence. We simply don't have the intelligence to even get close. Therefore, no matter what our imagination allows us to believe or understand about who God is, we will inevitably miss the real picture and miss who He is. Pride is said to be the biggest trap for humans and comes before a fall. Interestingly, the most enlightened and intelligent people throughout history admit that they don't know much or anything at all.

Personal Interpretation of Scriptures

People understand the Bible in several different ways. Some Southern religious groups handle rattlesnakes in church because it says in the Bible that men of faith will be able to "pick up snakes and drink poison without being hurt." Some preachers have died during this challenging learning experience after having been bitten.

There have been some modifications, missed translations, and removals done to the scriptures over and throughout the ages. Besides some changes not done purposely, some other changes were consciously made for political interests and to maintain power over the masses. But what is fantastic and what matters is that the essence and the main message have not changed over two thousand years. "God would not have allowed it," said Philostro.

During the Sermon on the Mount, Christ's message was in simple language for everyone to understand and a message most people and most religions of goodwill can accept and understand or should.

The most challenging and demanding concept is certainly the request to "love our enemy." This request is very misunderstood because of the many different personal concepts we have about an "enemy." What is easier to grasp and brings us closer to understanding is what Christ said immediately afterward: "For if you love those who love you, what reward do you have?" No one asks us to have positive emotions toward brutal dictators, but we can offer a little help to a neighbor in distress with whom we are quarreling. That neighbor might not accept our help the first time, but it creates miracles when they do so. Love is not about big emotions, but about the little unconditional helpers.

The historical description that Christ was conceived by the Holy Spirit through a virgin, resurrected on the third day after being put to death, and lifted into Heaven witnessed by his followers, remains a personal belief and is what defines a Christian.

Reincarnation

"As long as you are not aware of the continual law of Die and Be Again, you are merely a vague guest on a dark Earth."—Johann Wolfgang von Goethe.

Among historians, we can find the following regarding the impact of politics on the original Christian faith and its effect on the scriptures:

The Roman Cesar Constantine the Great, who reigned from 306 to 337, converted to Christianity and made it the Roman Empire's official religion, which is today the Roman Catholic Church. Constantine did have a considerable impact on the development of Christianity, as he reversed the general view of the gospels from being counter-cultural and mistrusted by the government to becoming the cultural standard of Europe, in alliance with government. Since the books in the Bible were not invented, modified, or corrupted by Constantine himself, we can use them to view Jesus and his Gospels that have been around since his disciples went forth proclaiming his message. Constantine was entirely in charge for a time (though he had plenty of help before, during, and long after death) of the creation of "The Bible" and his manipulation of the Church was also for political, monetary, and military reasons." Apparently, at that time, the most important passages in scripture dealing with reincarnation, which stated that humans go through multiple earthly lives, were removed. It is said that the reason for this was the dilemma of losing control over slaves because many could not be forced to work anymore as they would rather die, hoping to come back as a free person.

People are not dumb. Understandably, many do not believe that giving the simple lip service demanded by some churches will act as a sort of fire insurance to avoid burning in Hell. Consequently, many young people walked away from church, but the unfortunate part in doing so is to throw out the baby, Christ, with the bath water, the church.

The compelling need for humans to share and communicate together with and through a Divine Entity will inevitably create some kind of church. At the same time, the church needs to continuously evolve or even be completely renewed as time passes.

"Preach the Gospel at all times, use words if necessary," said Saint Francis of Assisi.

Why would God have created humans in His image, give them a single and extremely short time and chance on a single planet and then waste them for eternity by sending some to hell forever? Didn't Christ say that not one of his sheep will be lost and that the good shepherd with one hundred sheep would leave the ninety-nine by themselves, knowing that they were safe, and go after the lost one to save it from predators?

Christ also asked us to forgive. Why would God expect something from us He would not do Himself? Also, wouldn't it be incredibly selfish or prideful to see oneself in Heaven among the "good and saved souls" at the "banquet of the Lord" while simultaneously knowing about the bad guys burning in Hell forever? That can't work because this thinking is pure pride and selfishness, which has no place in Heaven. The childish concept of a single life followed by Heaven or Hell forever afterward, or purgatory if lucky, just does not work anymore. I believe some of the churches start to modify their approach, but the damage has been done.

At the same time, we cannot ignore the reality of the existence of Hell. How can we, as it exists in this world to a great extent? For the sake of simplicity, Heaven and Hell are explained in a mythological sense as places "above" and "below." For others, it is instead a state of existence. Two prisoners looking out the window, one looks up and wonders about the stars and the other one looks with despair down into the mud. With two people sitting on the mountain top at sunset, one is in awe of nature's beauty, while the other is complaining about the hike and fatigue. One looks toward Heaven and the other toward hell. What makes the difference? One is an old soul, the other a young one. Both could be of the same age with a similar upbringing, but one has many more experiences behind him than the other.

The age of the soul is defined by experiences over many lifetimes, not by earthly time. In this world, there are old souls in young bodies and young souls in old bodies. Philostro said that there are physical families and spiritual families.

To Live in the Present Moment

To live in the present moment has much less to do with clock or calendar time but more about living with awareness in the current situation. It is of course also awareness of the ongoing process and succession of happenings. Living in the present moment is not in contradiction to planning, which is related to a future time based on the clock or calendar.

What counts for humans is to be mentally present in the particular and current time frame, which allows us to physically or mentally act or react in accordance with what happens.

Life is more about how we deal with all the little things in each situation, how present and aware we are while doing so, rather than dreaming up great things, which is an illusion anyway.

Not living in the present moment is regretting or longing for the past and fearing or fantasizing about the future.

Living in the present moment is superbly described in *The Power of Now* by Eckhart Tolle.

Paradox

A paradox is only an apparent contradiction to our personal or collective world view and understanding at a given time. As we evolve through experiences and gain wisdom, paradoxes, vanish and are replaced by more challenging ones. It is proof of our inevitable personal evolution and, at the same time, of our limitations. Life is a mystery, and humans evolve very slowly. Therefore, it is wise to leave most mysteries of life to God and embrace our mythology. Philostro said not to dig too deep into the mysteries of life.

Suffering

Pain in Life is inevitable, but suffering is optional.

-Dan Millman

The main reason God accepts so much suffering and such turbulence in this world is that most of the time, if not all the time, the only way forward for us to discover true love, charity, and compassion is to go through painful journeys.

There is so much unnecessary inflicted pain to one another and to self in this world in the name of "righteousness." Righteousness is based mostly on religious dogmas; ones the adherents are willing to fight relentlessly for, with the desire to control others. There is a saying that no two people read the same book. Also, we understand the same text differently over time and as we gain more life experiences. That makes "righteousness" a personal opinion and becomes arbitrary to a certain degree. We should always question our perspective, and we can never be humble and tolerant enough toward other views. If we never modify or change our opinion, we are rigid, but life is movement. Life experience is movement and brings us progressively closer to Truth. It is essential to keep looking consciously for the Truth.

Geographical Values

Interestingly, very strongly opinionated people hardly ever walk their talk. Also, different cultures have different opinions about what is "good" or "bad." Sins are geographical to a great extent. Obesity is often pointed at very judgmentally in Europe, fortunately less so in the United States, where the problem is more severe. In America, cheating on your partner is harshly judged, while it is a lesser offense in Europe. The reality is that the consequences of gluttony and adultery cause the same problems everywhere, but pointing fingers adds insult to injury. Personal experience is what makes the difference in our tolerance levels. If we have been struggling with weight loss, no matter if we succeed or not, we will naturally restrain from criticizing others out of compassion. If we go through the experience of adultery and suffer the consequences, we will be less judgmental. Intolerance is what we have to apply to our personal misbehavior, and tolerance is what we have to apply to others' behavior. Forgiveness is what we must apply to ourselves and others.

Moral values have cultural and practical reasons at their origin. Some Saharan countries' biggest crime remains to steal a camel, as it most likely means the victim will die of thirst in the vast desert. It is still ingrained in the culture to a certain degree, even as automobiles replaced camels long ago. Horses in the Old West were essential for survival, and horse thieves were hung. Today, it is hard to give horses away. However, gratitude for their tremendous service in those days is still expressed through the respect we have for these animals and the fact that they are not consumed as food.

Forgiveness

The apostles asked Christ how many times they had to forgive their enemies. They wondered if it was necessary to forgive seven times, a mystical Jewish number. Christ replied that they have to forgive their enemies 70 × 7 times. In other words, we are supposed to forgive every single time and forever. If we are required to do so, and since we are created in His image, why would God Himself act differently? There is so much pain endured by humans caused by a lack of forgiveness, awareness, and education. Buddhist wisdom says that ignorance is a grave sin. More forgiveness would eliminate so much suffering in our world. There is an incredible true story showing the power of forgiveness in the book Left to Tell. It is authored by Immaculé Ilibagizia, one of two ladies who survived the Rwandan genocide in their hometown in 1994.

Duality

Physics is the most helpful branch of science to relate the laws of matter with the laws of spirit. Lately, Russian physicists have rediscovered, as several scientists in the world had done before, that our thinking has a considerable impact on our environment. In general, many seem to be aware that our thoughts impact other humans, animals, plants, and even water. Wouldn't that scientific "discovery" logically confirm the effectiveness of prayer, which is practiced in every religion?

In physics, there is no force without an equal counterforce. Advanced physicists say that the physical world is the reflection or the material realization of the spiritual world. Scriptures say that the battle is not in flesh and blood but in the spirit. We may look at the world just as a playground and battlefield for the physical execution and realization of spirit. Our world is only one of many, said Philostro.

Most religions believe that everything good, beautiful, and right comes from a Good God and Creator of all things. Bad, ugly, wrong, and untruthful things come from Satan, the devil, or Shiva, the god of destruction. Buddhism expresses this duality with yin and yang. Native Americans talk about the Great Spirit and the destructive forces leading us to evil actions. AA and Alanon groups, who do not want to embrace any specific religion, also realize that concept and describe it as the existence of a "Higher Power" versus "poor choices." Duality is the foundation of existence in this world and is represented in all cultures and religions. Day and night, light and darkness, male and female, in and out, up or down, hot and cold, good and evil, future and past are all realities in this world.

A New Age approach says that there is no duality and that everything is one. Certainly, yin and yang are represented in one circle, and good and evil are part of one Creation. There is also unity in diversity. Still, it does not neutralize or eliminate the reality of duality and polarity in itself. If we genuinely believe in a creative and loving God, we consequently have to also believe in a destructive and dark force. It does not matter how we want to call it. The word duality is often replaced or interchanged with polarity, because both indicate how all life on this planet is based on pairs and opposites.

To discount the leader of dark forces is spiritually one of the grand plans of the father of lies. To deny the divider is certainly also a reaction to the abuse to some of the teachings of the institutional church, trying to keep control by scaring the masses with eternal hell and the devil. The reaction and counter movement was inevitable, and to such an extent, that even many clergy members claim the nonexistence of the "devil" today. The word "devil" comes from the Greek language, diabolos, which means the divider, also translated as the slanderer or the back biter. Every conflict is based on "division." Isn't the name of this dark force very literal and explicative?

To ignore a hierarchy of dark forces is also a lack of wisdom and is detrimental to ourselves and against our spiritual benefit. How can we ignore a force which is involved in so many things humanity is doing?

Surely, there is no need to dwell obsessively on the Devil. The awareness of it is sufficient, but to discount it, is a philosophical luxury of a society living in high comfort and removed from the natural world.

Our personal opinions, based on our limited intelligence and knowledge, do not change facts, no matter how we call, see, or understand them.

C.S. Lewis, in his book The Screw Tape Letters, has a fascinating and humorous approach explaining the malice of the dark forces very well.

Philostro once asked a lady during one of his healing sessions what she would do if she had power over the devil. She said she would wring its neck. "That would be a grave mistake," responded Philostro.

The following might help us to understand his answer to that lady a little better: He also once said that a fallen angel who made it back up is superior and more advanced than an angel that had not fallen and remained innocent.

Spiritual insights are often explained and illustrated simply by most religions to make them accessible to a wide range of intellect. It is we who have a naïve interpretation most of the time. As a practical example and to better illustrate the advantage of a fallen angel who made it back up, take a person struggling with an addiction and who is looking for help. Who will inspire the addict more, the counselor who went through the same experience or the one who never did? We have to realize that the negative experience made a more enlightened counselor. In spirit as in the material, for the branches of life to reach higher toward the light, the roots also have to grow deeper into the darkness.

The concept of "Heaven and Hell" remains a personal picture, as everyone sees things differently. Some see it as a place and others as a state of being. It may also seem temporarily or ultimately irrelevant to some, but the consciousness of it is helpful.

Truth is not accessible by trusting our intellect with pride!

Missing: The Most Important Ingredient in our Food Chain

As already observed and concluded, the fundamental problem with our industrial food supply is the production of mostly lifeless food, with corresponding levels of toxins. This situation has its real and deep roots on a spiritual level. There is not enough kind and selfless service on every level of our industrial food chain! In other words, there is a lack of Love! At the top, personal profit overshadows the interest of the common good; the health of people, livestock, soil, and water. At the bottom of the food chain is a desperate, mostly undocumented, and abused workforce. At the end of the chain are also many restaurants worrying more about personal profit than food quality. Among consumers, there is too much ignorance, preference for convenience in the short term, and lack of education.

For some readers, the conclusion that our food system lacks love and compassion might be considered the idea of an idealistic dreamer. Still, most people will agree that the real problem of failing economies, low-quality production, and even reduced quality of life is primarily *greed*, which is a real, selfish, and negative spiritual trait. It is certainly not a technical or financial issue. Ask around, and you will find out. People in general are sufficiently intuitive and they will spontaneously give you the right answer. Simultaneously, we are humans with our weaknesses, lack of discipline, and our yielding to temptations. Sloth also contributes to our degrading food quality. Even in rural areas, it is challenging to find young Caucasian American people to do manual labor or fieldwork. Many would rather stay home and spend time on the screen or, paradoxically, workout at the gym because of a lack of exercise. We are simply not aware of the high price of "convenience" in the long run. The mental and spiritual sloth of refusing to face the problems we cause others and ourselves with irresponsible consumption and thoughtless actions is worse.

Politics

"It is not circumstances that need altering first, but yourself, and then the conditions will naturally alter"
—published by J.P Russell in *God Calling*.

Our problems cannot be solved technically, economically, or politically alone. There is no horizontal solution such as right or left for our human problems. Political and technical applications can only be successful after an altered mindset. The government is not the answer but an indispensable and necessary tool for a society to function. The government should be a workplace in the service of all. If enough individuals would be willing to change and be more of goodwill; if more individuals would have greater patience; would work and consume more consciously; provide and get a better education; teach and learn from honest science. . . the right political leaders and the right technical and political solutions would automatically emerge.

Just days before the outbreak of the corona virus, President Trump gave The State of the Union Address. Sometime later, the following message surfaced:

Thoughts about the State of the Union Address:

We are all different and have different points of view, which is good and meant to be. What is also meant to be is to work together. A State of the Union Address should be what it says.

Our forefathers created the Constitution based on Christian values, including respect for all religions.

Therefore, the following is addressed mostly to people of any Christian denomination and all others as well.

The President wants to allow prayer in public schools again. Hopefully, it will be a way to reunite us and is not just an agenda to gain additional votes. Nations without mythologies never persisted over a long period of time.

Certainly, some of the points President Trump presented were touching. Still, overall, the speech would have been more appropriate for a July 4th celebration. The main problems our country and the world are facing were not addressed, nor were solutions offered.

Pelosi's reaction to tear the transcript of the speech in pieces in front of everybody right afterward, while courageous and honest, reflected the Nation's division very well.

Again, as the President embraces religion and prayer, and since our Constitution is based on Christian values, let's compare the State of the Union Address's content with Christ's teachings.

Besides the eloquent feel-good, self-gratifying, and patriotic talk, the following principles and concepts of Christianity were missing:

- Humility: Christ said, "The first shall be last, and the last shall be first." He asked us to choose the seats in the back and to serve others; in other words: charity. Even a president can do that, just like some have done before. As it turns out, these men are still considered the best presidents in American history, for example, Abraham Lincoln.

- Honesty: Christ said the number one power tool of Satan is deceit. Philostro noted that if a person lies continuously, they do not know what truth is anymore.

- Fighting Poverty: Christ told us to practice charity and take care of the poor. Our major cities are experiencing an epidemic of homelessness while the stock market is skyrocketing for the wealthy. Rent is not affordable in big cities anymore, even for people with an education. Democracy?

- Taking Care of the Sick: We are the world's wealthiest country and the only one among modern industrial countries without a health-care system for all or even consensus that all citizens deserve access to basic health care.

- *Tending the Garden of Eden: God asked us to cherish his Creation and support all forms of life. He allowed us to use It but not to abuse It. We are destroying our environment and raping our beautiful country by treating it like a commodity. There was not a word about climate change! Science considers global warming mostly human-made. Personal emotions and agendas about that subject remain individual. They have nothing to do with what is happening and why it is happening. No words about the catastrophic fires, floods, and hurricanes that are increasing dramatically, especially in our country. Coincidence?*

- *Respecting Life: Christ said: "Who lives by the sword, dies by the sword." There is no mention of one of the worst epidemics of our time: Adults and children killed by mass shootings with assault weapons. Instead, we praise the "Holy" Second Amendment and the endless and hypocritical approach to abortion (which should not be supported, of course.) The father whose child was killed in a school shooting and who was in the audience, was very consciously ignored. Do we love guns more than our children or the children of others? The recent major demon–*

stration of extreme gun supporters in Virginia was on Martin Luther King Day. Coincidence?

- *Sharing: Christ said to use only what we need and not to store up riches. In America, three individuals hold the same equivalent net worth as the bottom 50 percent of US citizens. No word on our total wealth disparity and paying hard-working people a living wage. Democracy? Christianity?*

- *Love Your Enemy: Christ asked us to love our enemy. When we invade a country, we call it war. When some of these countries react in the ways they can, we call it terrorism. Certainly, there is real terrorism in this world that needs to be conquered, but let's use the correct words!*

- *Avarice and Gluttony: The number one killer and cause of premature death in the United States is the abuse of pharmaceuticals. Big Pharma often pushes unnecessary and dangerous drugs at exorbitant prices to serve their own profit, while recreational users die by the thousands, supporting drug cartels and the horrific violence associated with them. We are also a nation whose Food Industry does not care much about health, and whose Health Industry does not care enough about food. Huge chapters ignored!*

- *Unity: Was it really a "State of the Union Address"? If so, what is the plan to coordinate the wings of the Eagle? How much longer do we want to remain in this paralyzing state? When are we going to figure out that the only way is unity in diversity? The Eagle needs both wings to fly and to take off again. Don't both of our hands have to work together by giving and taking? It is not about endlessly lurching between right and left on the ground but about rising to higher levels. It is not about accusing others for our problems, but about changing ourselves. We are the only one we can change. It is certainly not about fighting over principals, but about applying them to ourselves.*

- *Confession and Repentance: Impeachment, absolutely no word about that?*

- *Request of Personal Effort: If too many trickles and little creeks are polluted, so the big lake will be, and eventually the ocean. Remember the request? "Don't ask what your country can do for you, but rather ask what you can do for your country." If enough of us serve others, we will have the government we deserve. We always have what we deserve.*

Americans are mostly descendants of people arriving from deprived and sometimes oppressed countries or situations. America's dream was to start anew on fertile and

222

almost virgin ground to provide freedom and prosperity for all and be an example for the rest of the world. Our ideals were set high. Perhaps the highest in human history. Our mistake is that we have largely failed to follow our ideals.

We are known to be Puritans, which is often a drawback because most things in life are not black or white, but something in between. One does not necessarily have to be a confirmed Christian to appreciate and apply human values and follow Christ's teaching. It was once said: "We are not humans who are meant to become spiritual, but spirits who are meant to become human."

There is no solution in politics because politics is not the solution. The snake cannot feed off its tail.

There is no journey to Happiness, Happiness is the journey.

There is no journey to Peace, Peace is the journey.

There is no journey to Love, Love is the journey.

If you want to be happy:

> *Be happy with what you have today.*
>
> *If you want Peace, be peaceful today.*
>
> *If you want Love, provide Love today.*

Love is to do to your neighbor what you wish done for you. It is to listen to your neighbor; it is to talk respectfully and gracefully about your neighbor; it provides the kind service needed, not more. Also be kind to yourself because the bar you set for yourself is what you set for others. Be the little

trickle of clean water that feeds the rivers and flows to the
ocean. Heaven takes care of the rest.

Climate Change

Temperature charts clearly show that average
world temperatures are rising considerably, which parallels the increase in fossil fuel burning. Already in the
late seventies, scientists from Exxon released that observation.

Interestingly, around the year 1900 Philostro said
that in approximately fifty years the poles would start
to reverse, and areas where it was cold would warm up
and areas where it was warm would cool down. As the
length of daylight has not changed and as a modification of the axial poles would require a massive physical
impact on the globe as we currently understand in
physics, it seems evident that Philostro was talking
about the magnetic poles. In recent years, scientists
have observed the rapid movement of the magnetic
North Pole drifting east from the Canadian to the Russian arctic at a speed of thirty to fifty miles per year. Scientists say that a total switch of the magnetic poles has
occurred several times in our globe's history.

Nonprofit-oriented science says that this very rapid
and recent warming of the planet is due to the human

activity of burning fossil fuels and releasing underground locked-in carbon into the air.

Climate change is a reality. Our responsibility is too important not to act upon it as much as we can. For many other reasons, such as air quality in cities, health, and pollution in general, humanity is invited to change to a better source of energy. There is currently more than enough scientific knowledge to make a big difference and get the work done.

An Evolved Form of Energy

The more our society evolves in a positive and human way, the more evolved our form of energy will be. A free and clean attitude towards one another will create clean and free energy. Polluted thoughts create polluted energy. Hopefully, our energy will become free of cost and available to all someday. We are not there yet. Not by a long shot, it seems. Sustainable energy, free of cost, would be the outcome of more evolved human behavior in our society. At the same time, it would become the expression of a fundamental and essential key to world peace. Free energy will only emerge when mutual respect in our society evolves. It goes hand in hand, but spiritual evolution is the forerunner to the material one. Current affairs do not seem to be going in a positive direction, though there is a lot of good being done in the background. At this moment, people in power seek to keep more and more control over the population. Everyone knows that we cannot keep going the same way much longer. It is important to realize that whole society has created the current system—no need to point at individuals.

The coal and steel industries were not interested in the free electromagnetic energy developed and demonstrated by Mr. Tesla in the early 1900s. Of course not, because it provided them no financial incentive and a loss of power and control. It would have put them out of business. Stanley Meyer from Ohio, who developed a water fuel cell and demonstrated how his vehicle ran basically on water alone, was assassinated. If both his invention and his assassination are as described on YouTube videos, it would be no surprise that his official cause of death was claimed to be a cerebral aneurysm and that the water fuel cells that powered his car were found to be fraudulent by an Ohio court in 1996. Anyone can study facts about cases like this, and everyone can make up their own mind. It takes an open mind, sufficient emotional distance, no financial attachments, common sense, and the capacity to put two and two together to figure out the truth in matters like this. A minority of people have that capacity because most of us were not educated in such a way. We need to keep in mind that the power of finances is almost limitless in this world and that everything can be bought, even "truth." If Stanley's water fuel cell worked, then an assassination is most likely the case. It follows that the destruction of this non-fossil fuel energy form had a huge impact on our society. As science claims that climate change or global warming is mostly manmade by burning fossil fuels, and if Stanley's water fuel cell worked, a combustion engine burning only water would actually be the miracle solution. Alas, humanity is still not ready for free energy despite all the severe warnings and existing knowledge.

The root of all human issues is always spiritual and can be on an individual or a collective basis. We are all created free agents, and we all navigate on the playground earth between good and evil. We are all scholars on our journey back to the Light. Of course, we bump into each other during that process. Spiritual confrontations on our path revolve around the seven dead ends: Avarice or greed by negligence or indifference to the less fortunate; Anger out of fear and control issues; Envy by stealing or racing for prestige; Gluttony expressed by eating disorders, alcoholism, and drug abuse; Lust by sexual abuse of others and self; Sloth by being unproductive nonparticipants and by living off others; and above all is Pride, by overestimating ourselves, our intelligence, and our capacity. We must learn to manage all selfish behavior during our apprenticeship and journey in this world and temptations are necessary to strengthen us on all levels.

Education

Another critical missing ingredient in our food production is education. Education about food intake starts when a baby is just a few weeks old. As children grow up, they have to learn the proper choice of food and quantity from an early age by example and regulation. Subsequent education has a lesser impact. Mothers knew how to feed their children a long time before any schools existed. I recall seeing an excellent talk show on TV a few years ago, speaking about psychology and different methods of educating children. One of the comments was that their education should start at approximately three weeks of age, right after the first critical period of adjustment of survival is complete. After that period, mothers should decide when to nurse their babies. The message was that the baby needs to learn to cope with frustration by letting the mother determine when it is time for nursing, not only the baby. As a child, I recall my mother saying so often, if not daily, when it came to eating: "That's enough." She always regulated our food intake and snacking. I recall observing the same in the families of my buddies.

Creation versus Evolution

Some problems in our society seem temporarily unsolvable because of misunderstandings, misinformation, lack of proper education, and critical thinking.

One of our acquaintances owns and manages a very successful woodwork shop and has several employees. He is equipped with top-of-the-line machinery, tools, and computers. He believes that the planet and humanity are 6,000 years old. That is what he understands from the book of Genesis in the bible. He manages a great business, is very talented and intelligent and had only seven to eight years of home-schooling.

On the one hand, he trusts and uses science by utilizing all its technology in his shop and for online work. On the other hand, he denies and rejects highly educated scientists and geologists who know how to precisely determine the age of matter with carbon14 and other proven methods. As we know, it is possible to determine the age of the individual and the period of time in which they died when found preserved in ice over tens of thousands of years. This skillful craftsman dismisses the scientific evaluation of our planet's age, which is supposed to be around 4.54 billion years old. Indeed, numbers that big are hard to grasp and quantify for most people. It is true that approximately six thousand years ago, something very significant happened in the evolution of human spirituality.

Strangely, most people decide to have either a purely scientific approach or a religious one. The endless debate between evangelicals and scientists over Creation versus Evolution is always a hot topic. It is an endless discussion between two types of stubborn puritans.

The question is, why should one exclude the other? "Creation is still in its doing," said Philostro, which means that the Creation is in constant evolution. Creation described in the scriptures as being completed by God in seven "days" should probably be understood symbolically as seven periods and not as calendar time. Many theologians from different churches support this idea. The genealogy of the scriptures from Adam and Eve to Abraham and all the way to Christ over six thousand years is not in contradiction with science. The theory that Adam and Eve represented the beginning of an important spiritual awakening for humanity but that they were not the first humans on the planet is *not* in contradiction with either science or scripture. After Cain killed Abel, it is stated that he wandered because he was afraid that other people would kill him as he killed his brother. Also, scripture says that he dwelled in the land of Nod east of Eden, where he met his wife. Who were these other people? Where did these people come from? Obviously, the world was already populated.

Education, critical, and logical thinking goes a long way but is not enough.

Humans, animals, plants, and all living forms change over time in looks and behavior. Some species die out, and some evolve quickly. There is a recent discovery of a bloodline of African elephants that are not growing tusks. Is this a genetically developing defense and a fast evolution of elephants to survive their poaching for ivory? It is likely since humans are the main predators of elephants. Some other animal species are adapted to various conditions and remain the same with steady DNA over tens or hundreds of thousands of years such as scorpions.

Philostro once said that in a cycle of twenty-four thousand years there is no spot on the planet that was not covered by water in one form or another. The proof is that we can find fossilized sea or water creatures on land just about everywhere in the world and at all altitudes. Isn't the only difference between Creation and Evolution the factor of time? Advanced scientists in physics say that time is a very relative thing. The concept of time is manmade, said Philostro. How can we debate Creation versus Evolution since our understanding of time is very vague and relative? The lifespan of a person happens in the blink of an eye compared to our planetary lifespan. If our globe's age, which is estimated to be 4.5 billion years, would be scaled down to one year, then an average human life span would be approximately 0.7 seconds in ratio. What an invitation to remain humble and instead marvel at this ever-evolving creation.

Opinions that are based on emotions and beliefs without any logic or scientific basis, such as pretending that the world is six thousand years old, are often and very sadly, violently defended. Again, we have always to be respectful and humble enough to consider that science and religion are not in contradiction, as it might seem. We just don't see it or have not discovered it yet.

The choice of an ideology and many personal decisions, and the purchase of goods, is often an emotional decision, not a rational one. The emotion is then justified with facts. Someone who knows how to sound convincing and how to "sell" their idea impacts many who are insecure and do not want to bother with rational thought and critical thinking. This inconveniently requires homework and education. Charismatic people often take advantage of that and abuse their gift to mislead the masses of simple and good people. It is a service to oneself and everyone to constantly question our thinking through continuous education and examining our consciousness and emotions. We must not let emotion take over and lead us to misbehavior and offensive language. To think and to be disciplined is inconvenient work, but these are the primary and powerful tools we have to work with in this world. Americans love convenience a little too much.

The Limitation of Science

Our "heart," the part of our being that lies somehow between Soul and spirit, is not from this world and is of much greater intelligence than our brain. The German poet Friedrich Schiller said: "Think with your heart and feel with your brain." Isn't it often said that the longest and hardest journey is from the head to the heart? It is good to realize that pride is the number one obstacle hindering that progress. Our decisions are, in their essence, not a result of our intellect or brain.

It is amazing how some sayings seem irrational, but they are actually proof of the Soul's language. We say, "This person has a good heart," which has nothing to do with the cardiovascular system. How about a "gut feeling" to express intuition or a person who has "balls" to express courage? Stumbling between good and bad decisions is not a matter of the brain. Some simple people do great things, and some brilliant people do horrible things. That is where purely physical-rational science hits a wall and its limitation. Traditional science will never be able to duplicate an Albert Einstein or a Beethoven. As genius as they were, it is not to be found in the genes, because DNA is malleable and formed by the spirit, not the other way around. Heredity is not of the body but of the spirit.

We capture pictures or templates which travel through space, something our brains cannot create independently; our brains are too weak for that, says Philostro.

In order to grasp new ideas, it is essential to let go of attachments and become liberated and free thinkers. By stubbornly or violently defending personal opinions, we most likely lose that faculty and that freedom to a large extent. We follow the flock. What makes great leaders who go against the flow of worldly ways? It is love and compassion for humankind, liberated thinking, and good behavior despite negative emotions. It is also a healthy curiosity and readiness to be continually learning. These are all spiritual qualities and not creations of the brain. At the same time, the thinking of great spirits is very logical and rational. When it comes to the significant limitations of science, the elephant in the room is, that science officially ignores the existence of God or a Creator and the eternal life of our spirits.

The Evolution and Transformation of Words

"In the beginning was the Word, and the Word was with God, and the Word was God. The same was in the beginning with God. All things were made by him" (John 1:1-3).

In the late nineties, during grand jury testimony, President Bill Clinton's responses were more than carefully worded as he argued, "It depends on what the meaning of the word 'is' is." Unfortunately, deviating from the truth by distorting words is a common strategy for some leaders to get their way, especially in politics. The majority of us ignore how much the public is lied to. By the way, the scandalous behavior of the media dragging the president through the mud because of his affair with Ms. Lewinsky was the bigger scandal. And the public highly supported the press. This particular lie became such a big deal because entertainment is more comfortable than focusing on what is going on in the country. Attention to real problems would require more homework from the receptor and more honesty from the emitter. Therefore, moral and financial issues such as lying, abortion, or taxes remain the electorate's primary focus. This simple factor remains a useful tool for politicians to deviate attention from other more critical and imminent matters. Political debates became entertainment. The politicians, leaders, and media who are focused on gaining something from the public for personal interest, are often very talented at wordplay. Jacques Delors, an exceptionally honest French politician who served as the eighth President of the European Commission from 1985 to 1995 minister in France, was asked why he did not want to run for president. His answer was, "because I am unable to lie." All this tells us that the choices and meaning of words have to be based on truth if we wish for constructive and honest communication.

It is a fact that over time the meanings of words are modified. Also, the relationship between words and individuals changes as we evolve. Words become problematic when abused or distorted for selfish reasons.

Powerful words such as love, marriage, and compassion have been challenged over time. For example, compassion is considered more of a feeling rather than the drive to action and help. Love has a more comprehensive range of meaning. Many words in our Western culture and philosophy are rooted in Ancient Greek.

For example, the Greek language differentiates four to six types of love:

1. Philia: affectionate regard, friendship;

2. Eros: mostly sexual passion;

3. Agape: charity;

4. Storge: tenderness, affection like between parents and children or also love for the country or a sports team;

5. Pragma: love demonstrated during a lengthy relationship, the practical type of love; and

6. Philautia: love for one's self.

Today the meaning of the word love ranges anywhere from promiscuity to self-sacrifice for others. The recent gay movement has brought an additional meaning to the *word* marriage. Same-sex marriage is in itself an oxymoron, but a legal union is necessary to establish civil rights for gay couples. Our society should not allow any negative judgment about same-sex couples. Still, the distortion and misuse of the word marriage is wrong. The few most important words that have kept the same meaning throughout human history should be maintained as such; otherwise, communication becomes a challenge and chaotic and will even lead to a deterioration of society. In Switzerland, same-sex couples may apply as a "Registered Partnership." This designation provides most of the same rights and responsibilities as in a marriage, except adoption rights, fertility treatments, and the right to adopt a spouse's surname.

To this day, American culture is still very much influenced directly or indirectly by Christian values with their traditions and language. Atheists, believing they have rejected all forms of religion, do not realize how much these values influence them and how much they live by these regularly and unconsciously. In Christianity, the word "Love" primarily means charity which is kind service and responsible actions towards one another. It is less a matter of feelings. Certainly, a feel-good side effect can be present, but it is hardly under our control. While it is impossible to have only positive emotions, even with people we "love," it is always possible to be kind and helpful to all who will accept it, even those we may be quarreling with. It is not complicated, but hard to do because it does not come naturally. It challenges our pride and short-circuits our spontaneous desire to react, intermingled with anger. Kindness often does not come easily and is not triggered by rationality but by compassion. Seen under that light, "love your neighbor as yourself" becomes a concept we understand better. It becomes a living statement.

The Evolution of Matter

Every farmer or gardener knows that manure stimulates and enhances the growth of plants. It is interesting to observe that what is useless and rejected by one category of beings is essential for the life of other less "evolved" types of beings. Alchemists describe the evolution of matter by saying that minerals need plants to evolve and plants need animals to evolve. On the other hand, vegetation feeds off minerals, and their elimination becomes food for the minerals. Ruminants feed off vegetation, and their elimination is food for the plants.

Ascending this hierarchy, it becomes less of a material matter. Does it help animals to evolve by being consumed by humans? Maybe, but most definitely, animals kept as pets and humanely raised livestock evolve by being around humans. And what do humans need for their evolution? Are we being consumed by God? Inevitably our lives and our development depend and are interconnected with God. We are at the top of the food chain and spiritual hierarchy on this planet. We are the only creatures given the freedom to choose between good and evil. Therefore, our souls need food that nurtures and grows our consciousness.

Our Daily Bread

History has shown that humans need mythology or spiritual food for existence, evolution, and survival. Without it, societies do not persist. This is the difference between us and the animal kingdom. So, let us embrace our humanity and freedom of choice by engaging our relationship with the Creator. The fact that we exercise judgment puts us at the top of the hierarchy and connects us intimately with the spiritual. This additional freedom provided to humans gives us access to powerful leverage. We have the option to either thrive and excel or commit suicide; to create or decimate.

Homo sapiens have physically evolved considerably over time, from cave dwellers to who we are now. Animals, on the other hand, have barely changed in looks and behavior over the same period. If they do change, it is for physical survival. We are the only mammal species capable of discerning consciously between supportive and non-supportive actions toward life. However, human souls may vary enormously from one to the other. Consequently, something has to make our soul grow over "time" or lifetimes. This growth is based on personal experiences during our earthly existences.

What kind of experience helps us to grow? Just as a bodybuilder needs resistance in the form of weights to grow bigger and stronger muscles, so does our nonmaterial self. Resistance or Opposition is fundamental and essential for growth; it is a life concept. We all know it consciously or unconsciously, no matter if we accept it or not. Don't we say that "what does not kill us makes us stronger" or "no pain, no gain"? The physical is the reflection of the non-physical, and spirit is over matter.

Our whole being is confronted with all kinds of little challenges daily. As we experience material life in this world, our spiritual battle is to resist the seven temptations. It is not about avoiding them but learning to live with them: to eat and drink and enjoy it, but not fall into gluttony; to own and to use what we need but to be liberated from greed; to control and to manage but refrain from angry actions; to enjoy sex without adultery or the abuse of the partner and oneself; to desire but not to envy; to create convenience without feeding sloth; to be aware of our qualities and a job well done without pride.

It certainly appears that there are more types of drawbacks than these seven traps. Still, all other wrongdoings or bad choices are rooted to one of them; for example, alcoholism is nothing else than gluttony, says Philostro. Is it a coincidence that there are seven days in a week, seven chakras, seven colors in the rainbow, seven frequencies in music, and seven Heavens like it is said?

Education and life experience are parts of our growing process, and so is resisting temptations. As we grow, we increase our capacity. Like an athlete who progressively adds more weight to his daily workout as his muscles get stronger, life will add more difficult learning lessons and will require more resistance in our daily routine. It is encouraging that we don't have to carry more than we can bear. Looking from our perspective at what some people go through in this world, it appears not to be true at times. It is because we tend to look more at physical suffering, which is often fatal. We are not supposed to be fearful of what may happen to our bodies, but rather what can happen to our souls.

Nourishment for our soul or "our daily bread" is light and truth, which we progressively achieve with the daily work required of us to do. The work required may not always be physical or mental activity. Our daily bread is also to be responsible toward all forms of life. Our beverage is the acceptance of the effort and strain, which goes along with that process. Is it a coincidence that top athletes who went through much physical exertion and pain are rewarded with a golden cup? It is essential to realize that the kind of experience, which makes us grow most is inevitably related to effort and resistance. Making an effort requires discipline and to move out of our comfort zone. There is no way around experience, good or bad. It is simply the setup of this earthly life. It takes most people at least one bad hangover to figure out the "right" amount they can drink. Growing (up) and rising to the occasion always requires effort, no matter our starting point, whether it is learning to walk or do vertical solo rock climbing, learn the alphabet, or attain a PhD. As our Soul evolves and gains "elevation," discovering new territory results in more consciousness and brings new joy and satisfaction to our lives.

The traditional concept in Christianity that we have to "suffer" to earn Heaven is unattractive in New Age thinking. "Pain in life is inevitable, but suffering is optional," says the Peaceful Warrior Dan Millman. This statement is more appealing nowadays since our understanding of the word "suffering" has somewhat changed over time. This statement also clearly implies that we don't "suffer" anymore once we accept the requested work or hardship. One has to endure much physical pain to become an Olympic medalist. No one is required to become an Olympic athlete, but they are great examples and teaching lessons for everyone. Fortunately, our daily bread presents itself usually in small rations, and that is sufficient for our growth.

In American culture, we have been encouraged not to judge. This is an excellent thing because we never know how much a person is carrying and how much pain they are enduring. Luis Ocana, a world-class cyclist who was the only one to have ever challenged Eddy Merckx and who won the Tour de France, had shown undeniable and tremendous efforts and focus on achieving that feat. The battle with alcoholism he fought a few years later, which lead to his suicide, was unknown to the public.

Our many little daily pains and difficulties are manageable. What is not manageable is the weight we add onto ourselves, mostly with the anxiety of tomorrow. Mark Twain once said that he was an old man who had known a great many troubles, but most of them never happened.

To endure resistance positively requires to freely pick up our load and heading up the path, rather than having to be constantly pushed. Cyclists in the Tour de France go through three weeks of very intense daily effort. Enduring the pain going up a pass, sometimes for hours, is real. But these men do not "suffer"; they accept a lot of pain for a bigger purpose. And once they reach the goal and stand on the podium in Paris, they have reached their Heaven. Their lives change, and they go on to the next step in their journey. The scientist who spends weeks, months, or years searching; sleeping and eating very little at times; spending the night on the bench in his lab isolated from social life, not knowing where his adventure of research is going to end, accepts all of that effort in the hopes of a breakthrough.

To successfully resist temptations without giving up, helps not only us personally but also others. It has many more repercussions than we think. We can read in the scriptures that the Lord said, "If I find fifty righteous people in the city of Sodom, I will spare the whole city for their sake."

Endurance includes the factor of time and will carry us to the next milestone, which is always encouragement and a release. Parents' patience with their teenage children and the acceptance to keep doing their best over the years is always rewarded one way or another. Parents do this because they know that it is for a bigger purpose and for their children to become successful adults. Once achieved with persistence, parents and their grown-up children become friends, or that's what it should be. The adolescent will also have to endure over this period and will have to forgive the parents for some of their wrongdoings if they want to grow up. To become an adolescent is to realize your parents are not gods, and to become an adult is to forgive them. Let's take more time and be more patient with one another.

The apparently grotesque concept that adversity is part of our soul food is a hard one to digest. But it is a reality of life. Our soul is not overfed forcefully but is forced to eat to live. Life or love seems to be almost forced upon us and makes growth inevitable, just as trees will add a ring of life after every season and become bigger and stronger every year. In that sense, Philostro's statement, saying that we all die as a better person than when we were born (because of suffering endured over our lifetime), should encourage us. It also indirectly indicates that we all have a different starting point in this particular earthly life and therefore have to have had past or previous experiences.

Life is good, and there is not only whole wheat bread but also cake. The soul also needs what goes down easy and which it will gladly receive. It can be the result of good works or simply a gift. It is manna for our soul when we are touched in any of its countless ways: healing of a disease; encouragement provided by others or by circumstances, the blessing to have confidence in the process of life, being forgiven, friendship, falling in love, the magical beauty and mystery of nature and the evolving creation, the gift of heavenly music and all kinds of art. It is a great gift to have a physical, intellectual, and spiritual appetite. Hunger is the great stimulus of life. Let's choose what feeds and helps us grow best.

Fortunately, intense pain is rarely present in most lives. Instead, beauty and the wonders of life are continually around us if we only lift our heads. We have the freedom to look at what we want to see. Our life's journey is a slight continuous uphill trajectory. We gain more altitude and a better view and vision of the landscape as we go and as we grow. We can choose steeper trails, and we do not need to carry heavy baggage that drains our force. We add unnecessary pain and stress to our lives by tackling too many unrequested things. Terrible additional and extreme pain is caused by feeding our addictions and our anxieties. Our day is designed so that all our little required efforts are manageable. It starts by getting up on time in the morning and is followed by a multitude of minor inconveniences intermingled with an equal number of blessings and good little things. We all have breaks and good times. A tough time is a time between two easy times.

Accepting the work put in front of us and doing what needs to be done, is part of our daily bread for the soul. Carrying the little pain which goes along with it, is part of our soul's beverage. Isn't that what Christ meant when he said to "eat this bread and drink this cup" in memory of Him and for us to have Life? Christians still commemorate this reality symbolically.

Love is the main ingredient feeding our whole being. If we do not accept this nourishment supplied to us and provide it to others, we become thirsty and hungry.

Disparities in Behavior

Much of our behavior is impacted by education, the cultural environment, and our landscapes. How can there be huge differences among people with the same upbringing or even within the same family? Why is it that even twins come into this world with sometimes pronounced differences in behavior? Couldn't the conclusion be that we come into this world with different baggage and different previous experiences? Are we born innocent? What makes one person compassionate and not another?

Let's look back at our personal life experiences. We discover that we can only be compassionate to someone's pain or problem if we have experienced approximately the same thing. We know it because we have experienced it at some point, and we are conscious of it. Experiences make us more aware, and difficulties or pain make us more compassionate and understanding. How is it that a young person with little experience, good or bad, can be compassionate toward the suffering of others? Was there an experience prior to this particular earthly life?

According to data released by the Pew Forum on Religion and Public Life (2009 survey), approximately 19 percent of the world's population believes in reincarnation. One-quarter of Americans believe in reincarnation, and it is the same ratio among American Christians. The highest percentage of Christians who believe in reincarnation, 40 percent, is found among young Catholics in Spain.

The main reason more people do not believe in multiple lives is simply that past life memory has been taken away from most of us. The very few people who have insight into this matter tell us this. Just as we arise in the morning and lose the memory of our dreams, the newborn baby loses the memory of where it came from. They also lose the capacity to see their guardian angel. More Christians have lost the knowledge of reincarnation, as mentioned before, because it was purposely removed from scripture in the early 4th century under Constantine of Rome. Leadership throughout the ages does not usually want people to know too much in general. Some passages in the scriptures reveal the existence of multiple lives, though. Solomon, who is described in the Old Testament as the wisest of all men, said: "I was born with a good body because I had been good before." Another indication is revealed when Christ was asked if John the Baptist was Elijah, an ancient prophet. Of course, any critic who does not believe in reincarnation will deny it with their scientific or religious arguments. As we are free to believe what we want, we still should find the courage to think on our own, keep an open mind, and question authority more often.

Isn't the possibility of multiple lives the only way to explain and understand the apparent injustice in this world? Why is someone born in ideal circumstances, good health, and surroundings, while another is born handicapped, in poverty and misery? If everyone would live only once, where would God's perfect justice be? The mystical author Paul Sédir said: "Injustices are justices whose causes we cannot perceive."

It is a widespread belief that everything happens for a good reason. Socrates/Dan Millman, the Peaceful Warrior, says in one of his books that whatever happens to us, good or bad, we deserved it. Philostro said once that he could assure us that we live many times, but we are certainly free to believe it or not. He also said that reincarnation is the only way to understand that we will pay for our shortcomings over several generations. A disabled man, who was born with a deformed lower back, came to one of Philostro's healing sessions.

Philostro took him aside and asked him if he knew why he had this problem. Of course, the man said he did not. Philostro told him: "In the 16th century, you were working for a wealthy owner, and you caught a neighbor boy stealing potatoes from the landlord's root cellar. You complained to the owner, but the landlord said to forget it, because a few potatoes were not going to make a big difference. Days later, you caught that same neighbor boy stealing potatoes again. You got very upset, and you hit him violently with a wooden post on his lower back. This assault caused him to be handicapped for the rest of his life. He and his mother went through great hardship because of that." Obviously, the disabled man had to experience the consequences himself to become a more compassionate person.

Fear and lack of faith, love, compassion, discipline, education, and wisdom cause us to fight in our households, with neighbors, and between countries. We may win a fight or a battle, but our enemy remains our enemy. It is an act of love, patience, and faith to convince an enemy who then turns into a friend. Opinions, expressions of feelings, and emotions contribute very little to peace and order in the home or country. Unfortunately, there is so much emphasis on these approaches today. Great people are known for their actions, less for their feelings, and emotions. Certainly, feelings and opinions need to be respected and valued. Still, our thoughts, words, and actions should not be dominated by them. We have to liberate ourselves from our personal enslavement.

Love, in other words, compassionate and kind service to one another, is the main ingredient to nurture body, mind, and soul properly.

Mentors, Leaders, and Teachers

Humans are not meant to be alone. We all need good examples and guidance in life, both food for our minds. Universal wisdom says that we are always at the right place at the right time and with the right people. As folks get older and wiser and look back on their lives and see how their lives unfolded, most will admit that. We cross the right teachers or mentors on our journeys when needed. As we grow and evolve, our teachers also change. Too many times we have to repeat the lessons unlearned. We then become teachers and examples for the people behind us. It is rare when we find an extraordinary mentor because the bulk of learning and teaching happens by our daily encounters with people around us. For most of us, our spouse is our number one mentor.

The boss at work has been placed there by life circumstances, which are of no coincidence. This hierarchy has to be respected. Philostro says that we have to do our very best to please and serve our bosses to the best of our ability. He also said that if we want to become a supervisor ourselves, we have to do more than what is requested to us when the boss is absent.

When it comes to national leaders, it is a human tendency to stay with the flock and follow a popular and charismatic person. Just as it is individually, societies or nations need leadership in one form or another. We have the leaders we need and deserve. We always do. Some leaders are indeed exceptional and will lift us up. Others will use and abuse us for their personal profit and interest. In both cases, they reflect the spirit of a nation as a whole. It is the politician's nature to act and react upon the strings pulled by its citizens. Politicians lead the country in appearance, but subconsciously and in reality, it is the people who lead politicians. That's why politics operates mostly on a horizontal level, right and left, rather than an ascendant one with real progress.

The direction leaders will bring us is very often not in accordance with what they said or promised. We can always recognize the tree by the fruits of its past actions. The fruits may be sweet or sour, or nonexistent, but it's never about eloquent speeches. This observation never fails when evaluating any leader. When it comes to politicians, we have to be very attentive to whom we attribute current successes or failures, due to short and continuous election cycles. This attention also requires personal homework, education, independent thinking, and critical observation to a certain degree.

Disputes and wars are often rooted in principles that people or nations do not follow or apply to themselves. So, let's do what we can do, control the one we can, which is ourselves, and by that, do the most we can do.

Where there is righteousness in the heart, there is beauty in the character. When there is beauty in the character, there is harmony in the home. When there is harmony in the home, there is order in the nation. When there is order in the nation, there is peace in the world.

– A. P. J. Abdul Kalam

Religion

To be religious does not necessarily mean to be spiritual or vice versa. It has been said that religion is the opium of the people.

The word religion comes from Latin. The most prevalent translation means Re-Ligare. Ligare means "to bind" or "to connect," and Re-ligare means "re-bind" or "reconnect." Greg Trimble says: "Religion is not a bad word. The definition of Religion in and of itself denotes peace and reconciliation. Religion does not encourage people to 'stop thinking.' In fact, Religion encourages people to think about how they can rebind themselves or reconnect with a God who is infinitely more intelligent and loving."

No nation or ethnic group was ever created or persisted without a mythology or form of religion. History shows that when a society eliminates their mythology, they vanish shortly after. That should make us think! Democracy, science, and secularism are not religions. What makes religion a "good or a bad thing" is like everything else. Religion can be used to support or destroy lives, to love or hate. Many wars and much suffering have been rooted in religion's abuse. Philostro recommended that we follow our religion. He said that all religions would melt into "one religion of charity" in the future; in other words, a religion based on mutual kind service. That sounds encouraging, and it seems like this process has started and will progressively increase, but not without cost. The "old" has to be partially stripped or pruned to allow new growth. When we prune trees and vines, the sap is flowing. Similarly, society will face difficult times or will even shed blood in order for something new to arise.

Change may come at a high cost to humanity but be beneficial in the long run.

Recently, the Notre Dame Cathedral in Paris burned down. It was a powerful message directed to France, which has become the most secular and profane industrialized country in the world. 40 percent of French people do not believe in God or a Supreme Being anymore. It was not an accident! It is an invitation and a cleansing to bring us back to real life and truth. The blow seemed to have also targeted the Catholic Church. It may be time to reconsider some of the teachings, outdated traditions, worldly power and abuses, all of which need to vanish.

France and many other countries have to reconnect with their mythology, look up to the Heavens again, obey the fundamental laws of life, and respect all forms of life. Hopefully, many got the message. John F. Kennedy's request to ask what we can do for America instead of what America can do for us can also be applied to the Church. Neither social democracy nor science is in contradiction to religion.

Prayer and Meditation

Scientists, mostly physicists, and lately Russian scientists, have discovered that our thinking impacts our environment considerably. The clairvoyant Christina Von Dreien of Switzerland states that if most of the world's population positively changed their thinking and attitude now, the world would change for the better in no time—within hours! The Japanese scientist Masaru Emoto shows how different frozen water molecules can look depending on their exposure to positive, kind human words and thoughts compared to negative and evil ones. He also shows the difference between water exposed to great classical music or heavy metal style music. The difference is astonishing. Check it out. It is worth it. All this is not surprising, and the scientific proof that kind words, meditation, and prayer work!

When torrential rain fell over France for an extended period during Philostro's time, he asked three friends to pray without ceasing about every bad thing they could think of for a couple of weeks so that Paris could be saved from serious floods. He also mentioned that people were not aware of the enormous volume of water existing underground. His three friends did their intense praying, the river Seine remained in its channel, the waters retreated, and the rain diminished.

We can approach this event with purely materialistic and rational thoughts and conclude that this outcome would have happened anyway and that prayers cannot be "proven." The difference in approach is spiritual and is based on faith, no matter the religion. The comment of Billy Graham's daughter should make us think. She was asked what she thought about the terrible school shootings our country had been experiencing in the past few years. Her reply was: "What do you think happens if you take God out of the classroom? You are on your own!"

It is essential to be aware of what we pray for. What are you hungry for? Is what we want ultimately good for us and our surroundings? We have to be aware that we can get answers to prayer from both sides of the spectrum, from "above" and "below." We have to be mindful that both sides listen, so we must consciously address our requests to God the Creator, the God of life, light and truth. We also have to be vigilant, ask for proper guidance, and not get confused because there are wolves in sheep's clothing. There are also "tough-love" guardian angels. It often seems that we do not get any answer to our prayers. We need to ask ourselves if our prayer was honest or if our request was selfish. Prayers are not always answered as we want because we only see part of the picture. Do parents always directly and immediately answer their child's every request, or do they always provide everything their children ask for?

One day a woman came to Philostro's daily healing sessions and asked him to cure her very ill son. Philostro seemed to ignore her, but after she came back twice and insisted, he said: "I will ask Heaven for your son to be cured but be aware that it was your wish." When she went home, her son was cured. Months later, she came back crying because her son had just killed her husband, his own father. The Lord's Prayer says, "*Thy Will be done*" because God knows what is best for us.

We don't know where we come from or where we are going. We know very little, so we might as well be wise and rely on the One who created, understands, and supports all life.

How do we know where the answer to our prayer comes from? Is it the right answer for us? Responses from both sides present to us in fundamentally different and somehow opposite ways. The Canadian Christian author Leandre Lachance explains that good advice arrives three times and can come from very different sources. He says that the right answers are not complicated, and that Heaven leaves us enough time to act.

To show our sincerity and for our prayer to be answered, we have to make a contribution. This may not look attractive or might seem hard to do at first. It might require courage and faith at times. Doubt is the weapon of evil and will make the necessary action seem too hard or too foolish to accomplish. Therefore, we may often avoid the required task. If the answer comes from

Heaven, it can be trusted and built upon because Heaven always keeps its promises.

In contrast, bad advice often seems very attractive, irresistible, and easy to achieve at first. It usually requires very fast or immediate action. Then it quickly becomes very complicated, more so as it goes on. It is often impossible to achieve or realize; it does not keep its promises, and the carrot continues dangling in front of our nose.

Heaven's help may sometimes lead one to worldly success. This help may be granted to the individual for the good of all. In that case, the concerned person remains poised, at peace, and detached from the outcome, considering himself or herself just as an agent. Suppose forces from below orchestrate our worldly success. In contrast, the person is restless, not at peace, attached to material success, and wants to control the outcome. The soul remains thirsty, and so it happens that very wealthy or successful people can also struggle greatly.

The answer to prayer can come in many different ways. It might come as advice from a friend. We might get the answer to our question provided in a radio talk show as we drive to work. The answer can be in a newspaper article or from a book we just started reading. Still, most of the time, the answer is the simple fact that particular doors open and others close, that we get rewards or have "accidents" or setbacks.

Regardless of religion or denomination, it is a general belief that God knows what is best for us and that we should ask for His advice above and before all. Philostro said that we should not ask for material privileges because all we need has already been prepared for us before our birth. Christ said: "Look at the birds in the sky, they do not sow and do not reap, and God provides all they need. So, if the Heavenly Father provides for the birds, how much more will He provide for you!"

A few years ago, based on a poll taken in the Bay Area of California, 85 percent of people who went from poverty or middle class to riches confirmed that they were not happier than before. But one does not have to exclude the other. There are poor rich people, and there are rich poor people. The difference is that spiritual people who enjoy a substantial income share it, create employment, often help the less fortunate and support all life forms. To be rich is when you need little!

Bill Gates is investing vast sums of money in Third World Countries with good intentions. The priest, Abbe Pierre of France, who died in 2007, was repeatedly voted France's most popular man. He was a humanitarian known for his work with the homeless. He was the founder of an extensive fleet of trucks that collected and redistributed household items for the poor while also building homes for the homeless. During that same period and ranking second in popularity, David Douillet was a two-time Olympic champion and four-time World champion in Judo heavyweights. After finishing his sporting career, he increased his popularity by engaging in the charity "Operation Yellow Coins." This is rich!

The mystical author Paul Sédir said: "Life is nothing else than Love, work and prayer." This may not sound very sexy or much fun for most young people. Therefore, this kind of life philosophy gets shoved under the carpet by a lot of us, despite its reality. If we think our life is only about bread and games, indeed the statement above makes no sense at all and seems counterproductive.

Playing and having fun is also an essential part of life, but it is not life's purpose. During one of his seven visits to the United States, Pope John Paul II said to us, "Don't play so much." Edgar Casey noted that "all work and no play" is destructive for us and those around us. These statements are not contradictory. The peaceful warrior Dan Millman says: "Work hard and play hard."

Life is more enjoyable if we focus well on what we are doing and do it consciously. Philostro said that it is better not to pray than to pray poorly. Doing one thing at a time makes life easier.

Life becomes tasteless and depressing when constantly distracted.

Here again, the word prayer has lost its meaning in our consumer society. The ideology of self-interest has distorted the profound sense of this word. The word "meditation" is more utilized today. Meditating is a beneficial and necessary practice to interiorize our minds and thoughts. Eastern cultures have greatly influenced the practice of meditation, which mainly focuses on self. It helps to relax, enhance self-awareness, and manage distress and anxiety. Perhaps New Age philosophy over-emphasized meditation to some extent. Swami Vivekananda, a key figure in the introduction of Indian philosophies to the Western world, said that five minutes of meditation a day is enough and that the rest of the time should be action.

Prayer instead emphasizes a personal relationship with the Creator. The word prayer comes from the old French "prier" whose roots are from Latin and means to ask or beg. When confronted by extreme hardship, we realize our vulnerability and relative nothingness in this world and our total dependence on the Creator. This is the moment we start to ask or beg. Prayer and meditation have an essential common denominator and are not separate activities. Both are essential and related to God. Prayer is active and meditation is passive, which is not meant in a negative or positive way, but in its form and direction.

With the COVID-19 pandemic, we realize our vulnerability. Dead bodies are pushed out of the hospital and buried or cremated without their loved ones' participation in burial and grieving rituals. There are no atheists in the foxholes, but prayer is as critical during good times.

Prayer is a direct, personal, active connection and type of request to the Heavens and does not have to be recited in ritual form or in a particular place. It can be expressed in different ways anywhere and anytime but requires an open heart and honesty. Prayer is also gratitude for all the gifts of life and the blessings received. Gratitude is best expressed by giving back to all forms of life. Giving back is not about planning great projects, which we often can't and won't accomplish. It is about engaging in all the possible daily actions presented to us.

To do unto others what we would like to be done unto us. It is to accept the work we have to do and to do it as well as possible. It is about accepting new upcoming life. It is to refrain from bad-mouthing others. It is the little things that matter: doing the dishes; helping a neighbor; giving a generous tip to hard-working waiters and waitresses; providing food waste to hungry birds and animals, etc.

Prayer, meditation, discipline, and conscious effort are vital tools for a beautiful and intense life!

The Fear of Hardship

Daily problems and difficulties are always more significant in our minds than in reality. Even though our day was manageable and relatively pleasant, we often tend to complain, and we spoil it. The thought of doing a polar bear dip is more challenging than actually doing it. The hardest part about going for a run is getting out the front door. Growth is accepting the process of necessary constructive work that often requires effort.

The more we move toward obeying the rules of life and accepting specific facts of life, the more peace and joy we have.

Years ago, I recall seeing a nervous young man at bingo night. He was aggravated and unhappy because the numbers didn't turn out the way he hoped. At the next table was a seriously disabled young lady in a wheelchair, forced to use the marker with her mouth. She was radiant with joy and happy to be at the bingo game that night! Watch the severely handicapped Paul

Smith from Oregon doing his marvelous paintings with an old typewriter and one finger. The man is radiant, and he makes people happy around him.

Have you ever seen the motivational speaker Nick Vujicic, the man without legs and arms? Google his name or put in "no arms no legs," then ask yourself if you really had a bad day, if your life is too hard or if you are "missing" something.

Fun

Fun in life is necessary. It helps fortify relationships, is relaxing, and is time spent together, vital for strong family connections. As we know, there is also such a thing as having "too much fun" with the consequences that follow. The pursuit of fun is like everything else in life: moderation is key. Too much fun, just like abusing alcohol, leaves a person feeling numb and unsatisfied, among other things.

Unfortunately, fun became a consumer item in current times. It seems to have priority over everything else and overshadows every other value. Commercially, it became the purpose of life. Everything is supposed to be fun. Having fun snacking rather than nourishing ourselves; taking medication instead of changing lifestyle; making faces on each selfie instead of connecting with one another; spending money frivolously instead of saving for good purposes; and having casual relationships over enduring commitments. My brother said, "All ads on TV are showing us how to become happier if we only purchase the product. It goes on nonstop. We are supposed to buy everything to get enlightenment and ultimate satisfaction, but leave mountains of waste, injustice, and a toxic environment."

When the Presidential candidate Joe Biden chose Mrs. Kamala Harris as a potential Vice President, many rejoiced. The proof that she seems to be a very respectable lady is that several members of the Republican Party also congratulated her. However, one of the comments overheard was a politician's final words addressed directly to her: ". . . and have fun!" Really, in our day and age and the situation our country finds itself in now?

Fun is related to a pleasant, exciting, and relatively short-term physical feeling. Fun is fast to come and go.

The desire for more fun nowadays is probably also a reaction to its prohibition imposed by some religious directives generations ago. To have fun was almost a sin in many religious circles. Unfortunately, many churches use fear and guilt to manipulate and control their members, leaving little room for self-expression in the form of fun.

God wants his children to have some fun and share plenty of good times and laughter, but He does not intend for it to be the goal and the purpose of life.

Happiness

Is the purpose of Life to be happy? It may be a goal and a civil right mentioned in the Declaration of Independence, but it is not the purpose of this earthly life. Happiness is more associated with a satisfied mind. Happiness is more mellow but more enduring compared to fun.

The contemporary English novelist Zadie Smith says: "Happiness is not an absolute value. It is a state of comparison." Doesn't comparison also create poverty to a certain extent? Years ago, I listened to a radio interview about a doctor who volunteered somewhere in the Far East Mongolian mountains. He described how these people lived very simply, attending their small herds of animals and gathering in simple homes without running water or electricity. There were no asphalt roads. This doctor was stunned to see how happy these families were and how well they lived together. He realized that they did not know anything different. After several months, coming back home was a wake-up call for him to see kids sitting unattended in front of the TV, watching commercials showing them all the things they didn't have. He concluded: "That is poverty!"

The French philosopher and author, Albert Camus, who won the Nobel Prize for literature in 1957 said:

"What is happiness but the simple agreement between a being and the existence that it entails? You will never be happy if you continue to search for what happiness consists of. You will never live if you are looking for the meaning of life."

Joy

Joy is to know that we belong and that we are loved; that our needs are and will always be met. It is to know that we are safe and always protected. That we are never alone and that we all have a special place in this creation. Joy is to be living in the present moment because we trust the process and do not worry about tomorrow. It is having the capacity to be in awe of and marvel at the beauty of this continuously evolving creation around us. It is to know with certainty that despite our differences, we are all One.

Joy is the docile and calm state of a satisfied soul. It is the only state that can last over our entire life span. There are many words to describe fun and happiness, but only a few to express joy.

How does joy differ from happiness? They have partially common ground. That is why there is sometimes a bit of confusion between the two. Happiness is more of a physical and mental state and usually triggered by our environment—home, income, activity, relationships, weather, places, events, etc. Joy is a state of the soul achieved mainly by the acceptance of life as it presents itself and obedience to its laws. It is to be in accordance with our consciousness at the present time. Accepting how we are and how we live physically adds to happiness while accepting how life presents itself to us adds joy.

In their inspirational book, God Calling, edited by A.J. Russell, two anonymous British ladies say: "Joy is of two kinds. The Joy born of Love and Wonder and the Joy born of Love and Knowledge, and between the experience of the two Joys lie discipline, disappointment and almost disillusion."

Joy has a gentle, profound, and radiant smile, while happiness laughs and fun giggles. When in a state of joy, fun, and happiness are of no concern.

Similar to the existence of body, mind, and soul, the states of fun, happiness, and joy are not entirely separate from one other and do affect one other.

The Responsibility of Pursuing Happiness

Of course, we all want life-intensity. When the wind is blowing straight into our sails, life feels good, but that does not mean it is good for everyone. It depends on what direction we are heading. Our fast and intense pace and behavior may negatively impact people, animals, plants, and the environment. Does our achieved life intensity help and inspire others, or does it discourage them? If pursuing a selfish drive recklessly, it will bring us down as well, sooner or later. It is just a matter of time.

In business, win–win situations are deals providing durable and real growth. Sales that serve only the salesman and his company usually do not provide lasting fruits. We have an inherent and God-given trait within us: we cannot really be happy or joyful in the long run if our partner, family, neighbors, friends, or colleagues are not happy also. We have a God-given desire to share our joy with others. And that is the clear indication and proof that others matter! Others matter as much as we do and sometimes more. Selfishness is a dead end with a short life span. Indifference to the suffering of others is worse than hatred itself.

It is a lack of consciousness due to a lack of compassion caused by a lack of difficult personal ex–

periences. A wolf killing sheep has no compassion, no consciousness about the pain it causes. As humans, we are called to a higher purpose; although we are not humans who are meant to become spiritual, we are instead spirits who are meant to become human(e). This helps us understand why an emphasis on personal profit is detrimental to our society and ultimately to ourselves and has no chance of persisting. Unfortunately, personal financial gain and selfishness have been almost a religious focus of our nation for too long now. COVID-19 is an invitation to think this through again but may not be enough to turn things around sufficiently. In general, we are very short-sighted, irrational, and illogical. Without change, we will inevitably open the door to additional hardships of all kinds.

Kindness, generosity, and compassion provide joy to the giver and receiver. There will always be work, but the pursuit of personal gain and hyperactivity remains optional.

Joy is the outcome of obedience to God, the adherence to what is good, right, and beautiful to all forms of life in the present moment.

Spiritual Quest

On my last trip from Europe coming home, I watched a breathtaking documentary done by National

Geographic about Alex Honnold, who became the first climber to do a free solo up Yosemite's 3,000-foot El Capitan wall. To watch this young man climb vertical rock walls thousands of feet above the ground without any safety will make you dizzy but amazingly won't and can't make Alex himself dizzy. Even the climbers filming the scene from the flat ground had to turn their heads away at times.

Our material world is a mirror of what is going on in the spiritual world. Our spiritual quest is comparable to ascending a mountain top in search of light, vision, accomplishment, and freedom. There are many ways to get there, or as the old saying goes, "All roads lead to Rome."

Very few chose steep and dangerous spiritual paths. Our God-given freedom allows us to select our personal path, and life gives us a wide range of options as long as we continue moving. A majority pick the well-traveled paths. No one, with the exception of God at times, can impose on us which path to take. But life is calling and demanding us to ascend! It is a call that attracts us if we keep our hearts and eyes open and a call that pulls us up if we accept help and love. It becomes a push if we refuse to move and it will consequently feel like enforcement and restriction. That is when we start to "suffer" and feel sorry for ourselves, become unhappy and find no more joy in life.

There are many ways to ascend the mountain. These range anywhere from the long, gentle uphill on the safe trail to the straight steep solo climb and any option in between. Whatsoever, our journey must be adapted to the nature of our being and the state of our evolution. When on our spiritual quest, we most likely won't be an Alex. If our pride leads us to a steep and dangerous ascent, we run the risk of a severe setback or fatality. Pride comes before a fall, as we know. Many "saints" fell into that trap! And no, as much as this idea circulates today, we cannot become anything we want to be. With our heads in the clouds, faith, and good works can take us further than expected, but we need to remain humble and keep our feet on the ground.

We need to be aware of our appetite and what we are hungry for but be careful not to choke while biting off more than we can chew.

Final Words

If you came this far in the book, you most likely encountered some new and thought-provoking approaches. Some things may not make sense to you at this moment in time; some never will in this lifetime, and some may be impossible to believe or just seem plain weird. That is perfectly fine. Some approaches do not match the accepted doctrines of science or religious beliefs of this world. We eat the spiritual food that suits us best and shouldn't bite off more than we can chew, but getting the taste of something new can't hurt and may open the door to new journeys.

The book is not about convincing anyone of anything, but much more about sharing and mutually expanding our horizons together by looking at what would be for many a different map and which may help us discover unknown territories. This map does not show different landscapes but maybe unknown routes and trails. As usual, the one who benefits the most from this kind of map is probably the designer himself. The book might help us to change course and get more wind in our sails. It may be an invitation to travel on our own sometimes and discover the tranquility, peace, and new enlightenment that solitude can offer. But it will also create new and different hurdles and new challenges because we are responsible for what we know. We all need to expand our capacity to think outside of the box, let go of habits, thought patterns, and negativity, and forgive by trusting and unloading unnecessary burdens such as anger, anxiety, or addiction, all weighing heavily on our shoulders. There is so much more to life than what meets the eye, and at the same time, there is much more to do than to know. This book may help you realize that we grow more through experiences than through knowledge, but both are essential for our evolution because we need to educate ourselves as much as possible while actively looking and asking for answers to our questions.

At the end of life, we will hopefully realize that it is not so much about what we believed but more about what we did and how much we have loved, served, and participated in supporting all life forms, including our own.

Let us open up to life and predominantly use our hearts to think rather than our heads. Let us embrace life by thinking courageously and independently rather than giving that ability away to others or authorities. Let us be aware that we are all One on some level, that all is One, but realize that we are all different and that there is a hierarchy in the spiritual world and, therefore, also in the physical world. Let's give ourselves and others a chance to rise, grow, and evolve because the world needs it so badly. The world situation will only improve if the majority of individuals will improve, which means improving ourselves. If something does not work, change will help us get further because life is movement. But resisting will drag us further down because rigidity is death. We humans desperately need help, we depend on it, but we also have to accept it and do something in return for it. We need help that is beyond our capacity, and we depend entirely on the support of the One who created us. To honor Him is to obey Him and cherish all forms of Life, to appreciate the right to use it without abusing it. For that, we need to find our mythology and nourish a personal relationship with the entities from Heaven who try to help us. We can do this by following our religion. We also need to read the book God has written: Nature. Let us realize that life allows us to do whatever we want as long as we love, as long as our actions respect all forms of life we are aware of, and as long as we are obedient to the rules of Truth. The time is now, and the place is here, says the Peaceful Warrior. And as Philostro said:

"Remember that time is very valuable!"